Called to Compete: Faith-Driven Devotional for Female Athletes

Christian Sports Devotions to Build Mental Toughness, Discipline, Navigate Pressure, & Develop a Growth Mindset

NextLevel Publications

Contents

UNLEASH YOUR POTENTIAL

Excellence in sports has never been limited by gender. Across arenas, pools, fields, and courts, female athletes continue to redefine strength, leadership, and influence. Behind many of those competitors is something unseen but unshakable—a faith that steadies them when pressure rises and expectations grow louder.

At the highest levels of competition, countless athletes have discovered that confidence rooted only in performance will always be fragile. What lasts is a deeper foundation—one built on trust in God, humility in success, and perseverance through adversity. This devotional was created to cultivate that foundation in athletes who want to compete with clarity, courage, and conviction.

Consider athletes like Katie Ledecky, whose historic career has been marked by consistent gratitude and reliance on God rather than applause. Gabby Douglas carried her faith onto the Olympic stage when the spotlight was brightest. Alyssa Naeher leaned into God's strength while bearing the weight of World Cup expectations, while Jennie Finch used her platform not only to excel in her sport, but to invest in the next generation through her faith.

What set these women apart was never talent alone. Their impact came from resilience developed in unseen moments, humility practiced in victory, and confidence anchored in Christ rather than outcomes. That is the heart behind this devotional.

Called to Compete: Faith-Driven Devotional for Female Athletes is designed as a weekly rhythm of spiritual conditioning. In the same way physical training builds endurance over time, these short devotions are meant to strengthen faith, sharpen focus, and reinforce values that carry over into competition, leadership, relationships, and everyday life.

Each week follows a simple, purposeful format:

- **Scripture Verse** – A focused passage to anchor your week in God's Word
- **Scripture Insight** – A brief breakdown of the verse that highlights how God's Word shapes your mindset, habits, and approach to your sport.
- **More Than the Scoreboard** – A concise lesson drawn from real experiences of professional female Christian athletes and teams
- **Pathway to Growth** – Thought-provoking personal reflection paired with a practical faith-in-action challenge
- **Quiet Prayer** – A brief prayer to reset your heart and realign your priorities
- **Notes** – Space to reflect, process, and record what God is teaching you

These few intentional minutes each week are designed to help athletes compete with purpose, navigate pressure and comparison with peace, develop Christ-centered mental toughness, and lead with integrity on and off the field.

Your sport and talent are gifts—but your character and influence are what endure. This devotional exists to train the heart alongside the body, helping you pursue excellence with purpose and a foundation that cannot be shaken.

HOW TO USE THIS DEVOTIONAL

1. Short Devotions, Just for You: Each devotion is designed to take about one or two minutes. Read one devotion at the start of each week – in the morning, before practice, or whenever you need encouragement. You don't need a lot of time. Just show up.

2. Put It into Action: Every devotion includes a personal reflection, faith in action step, and a quiet prayer. It might encourage you to think differently, act with courage, or show kindness. Small steps, taken consistently, build confidence and faith over time.

3. Talk to God Honestly: Each devotion ends with a short, impactful prayer. Talk to God about what you're feeling, what you're hoping for, and what feels heavy. He cares about every part of your life, on and off the field.

4. Progress, Not Perfection: You don't have to be perfect to grow in your faith. If you miss a day, don't stress. Pick it back up when you can. God's grace meets you right where you are, every single time.

5. Share the Encouragement: If a devotion speaks to you, don't keep it to yourself. Share it with a teammate, a coach, a friend, or a family member. Encouragement is stronger when it's passed along. Remember, you are always loved and never walk alone.

SECTION 1: ROOTED IN FAITH

(Weeks 1 - 16)

This section focuses on establishing identity where it truly belongs—in Christ, not in performance or statistics. It emphasizes that lasting leadership in sport begins off the field, shaped by faith, character, and spiritual grounding long before results are visible.

These opening devotions guide female athletes in strengthening their identity in Christ, developing humility and gratitude, embracing self-respect, and competing with integrity. Together, they lay a firm spiritual foundation that supports both athletic excellence and a life that honors God.

CHAPTER 1: YOUR PURPOSE, HIS GLORY

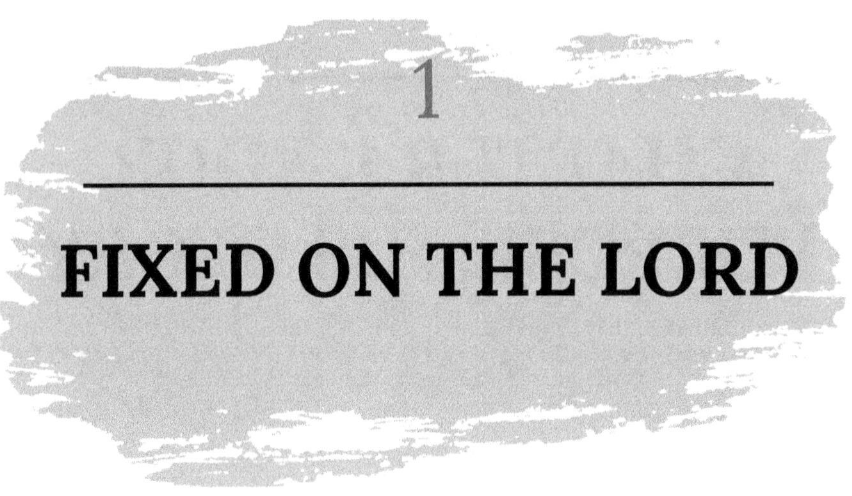

1

FIXED ON THE LORD

"I keep my eyes always on the Lord. With him at my right hand, I will not be shaken."
Psalm 16:8

Scripture Insight: Psalm 16:8 speaks to the kind of focus that holds steady under pressure. Keeping your eyes on the Lord means choosing awareness of His presence over the noise that surrounds competition—expectations, nerves, comparisons, and the desire for approval. When attention shifts away from God, instability follows; when it returns to Him, confidence settles in.

In sport, focus determines direction. Just as an athlete fixes her gaze to maintain balance and momentum, faith calls us to center our hearts on Christ. This verse reminds us that steadiness does not come from control or performance, but from knowing God is near and actively involved in every moment.

MORE THAN THE SCOREBOARD

Athlete Spotlight: At the professional level, expectations run high, yet **Mallory Swanson** has learned to anchor her confidence in Christ rather than performance. As a forward for the U.S. Women's National Team, she has faced injuries and competitive setbacks that could have shaken her identity.

Instead of letting goals, minutes, or public praise define her, Mallory consistently redirects attention to God. She has spoken about playing for the Lord and using her gifts to honor Him, recognizing that soccer is not the source of her worth.

This posture allows her to compete boldly and stay steady whether she scores or struggles. Mallory's perspective reflects the truth of Psalm 16:8—when your eyes remain fixed on the Lord, circumstances lose their power to shake you. Her example shows female athletes that real confidence and glory belong to Christ, and giving Him the glory transforms how you play and how you live.

PATHWAY TO GROWTH

Personal Reflection: *What tends to pull my focus away from God when pressure increases? Where have I allowed outcomes or opinions to carry more weight than His presence?*

Faith in Action: Before your next practice or competition, take a quiet moment to acknowledge God's presence with you. Instead of repeating the entire verse, choose one phrase—"*I will not be shaken*"—and let it guide your focus. Throughout the week, practice redirecting your attention back to God whenever distractions surface, allowing Him to steady your mindset and shape how you compete.

Quiet Prayer: God, thank You for being near in every moment, whether seen or unseen. Help me keep my focus on You when pressure rises and distractions compete for my attention. Teach me to compete with confidence that comes from Your presence, and to honor You in both victory and challenge. **Amen.**

NOTES

2

YOUR DEEPER WHY

"And we know that in all things God works for the good of those who love him, who have been called according to his purpose."
Romans 8:28

Scripture Insight: Romans 8:28 tells us that nothing in our lives is accidental or wasted. God is actively at work through victories, disappointments, delays, and detours, weaving each experience into His greater purpose. This truth reshapes how we view our journey as athletes. Even moments that feel confusing or costly can serve a meaningful role when our lives are aligned with God's calling rather than personal outcomes alone.

MORE THAN THE SCOREBOARD

Athlete Spotlight: Ruthie Bolton reached the heights of her sport as a two-time Olympic gold medalist, WNBA pioneer, and an anchor of Team USA. Yet as her platform grew, she sensed God calling her to something deeper than basketball's success. Winning alone did not satisfy the purpose He was shaping in her.

That realization changed how she viewed her influence. Ruthie began sharing openly about trauma, restoration, and the hope she found in Christ. She stepped into ministry roles as a speaker and mentor, using her story to encourage healing and point others toward Jesus. The court became a starting point—not the destination.

Her life reflects the truth of Romans 8:28. God used both her victories and her wounds to form a testimony that reached far beyond sports. Ruthie's journey reminds athletes that purpose is not limited to titles or statistics. When we trust God with our story, He brings meaning that outlasts our career and impacts lives we may never see.

PATHWAY TO GROWTH

Personal Reflection: *Where do I sense God inviting me to think beyond performance and results? In what ways could He be using my experiences, discipline, or influence for a greater purpose than I currently see?*

Faith in Action: Set aside time this week to identify one intentional way your sport can become a channel for service. Rather than focusing on personal outcomes, choose an action that benefits others—offering encouragement, stepping into leadership, or using your voice to reflect Christ. Let your choices communicate that your purpose is larger than competition alone.

Quiet Prayer: Gracious God, thank You for designing my life with meaning that goes beyond wins and losses. Help me recognize how You are working through every season, both seen and unseen. Guide me to use my gifts with courage, humility, and faith, trusting that Your purpose is always at work. **Amen**.

NOTES

3

THE UNFADING CROWN

"And when the Chief Shepherd appears, you will receive the crown of glory that will never fade away."
1 Peter 5:4

Scripture Insight: This verse directs our attention beyond temporary recognition to a reward that lasts forever. Jesus, described as the Chief Shepherd, promises an eternal crown to those who faithfully follow Him. While medals, trophies, and titles carry meaning for a season, they eventually lose their shine. The crown Christ offers is unchanging and permanent. This truth reminds us that the greatest victories are not measured by applause or public recognition, but by a life lived in obedience and honor to God.

MORE THAN THE SCOREBOARD

Athlete Spotlight: Jackie Joyner-Kersee is recognized as one of the greatest track and field athletes of all time, earning multiple Olympic gold medals and world records across the heptathlon and long jump. Her excellence drew global attention, yet she consistently viewed her talent and opportunities as gifts from God rather than personal achievements to claim.

As her career unfolded, Jackie redirected a portion of her success toward serving others. She established the Jackie Joyner-Kersee Foundation to support youth and families in underserved communities, demonstrating that influence used for God's purposes carries more weight than any medal count. Her faith shaped not only how she competed, but how she cared, mentored, and invested beyond the stadium lights.

Jackie's journey reflects the message of 1 Peter 5:4. Earthly awards are meaningful for a moment, but they eventually lose their shine. The crown Christ offers to us endures beyond every podium and public celebration. Her example reframes victory for female athletes: honor God with what you've been given, and the greatest reward will never fade.

PATHWAY TO GROWTH

Personal Reflection: *Which achievements or forms of recognition do I tend to value most in my sport? How does the promise of an unfading crown reshape my understanding of success?*

Faith In Action: After your next practice or competition, pause before moving on or sharing the moment with others. Take time to acknowledge God in prayer, intentionally giving Him credit for the strength, opportunity, and ability you were given. Let your words and actions communicate that honoring Christ matters more than recognition.

Quiet Prayer: God, thank You for the gifts and opportunities You have placed in my life through sport. Help me remember that medals and trophies fade, but Your promises endure. Teach me to give You glory in every season, trusting that the greatest reward is found in living for You. **Amen.**

NOTES

CHAPTER 2: IDENTITY BEYOND THE MIRROR

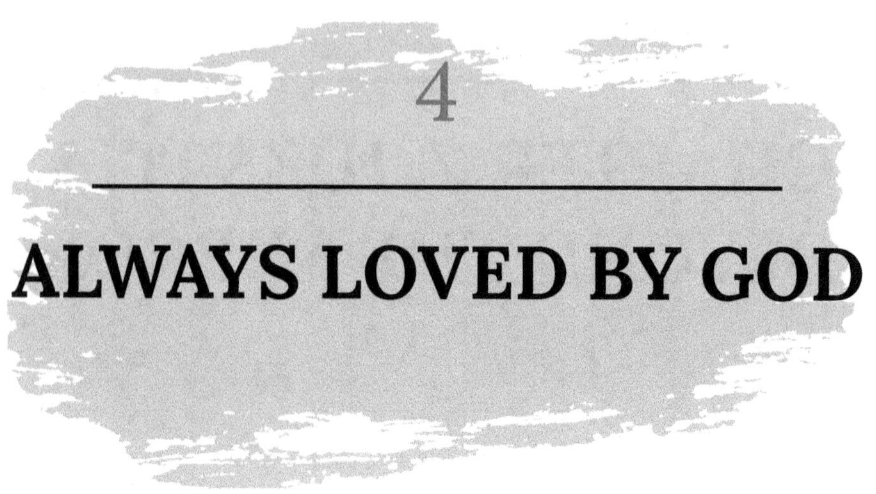

4

ALWAYS LOVED BY GOD

"Am I now trying to win the approval of human beings, or of God? Or am I trying to please people? If I were still trying to please people, I would not be a servant of Christ."
Galatians 1:10

Scripture Insight: Galatians 1:10 confronts a tension every athlete faces: living for approval versus living for Christ. When the drive to satisfy others becomes the priority, faith slowly loses its place at the center. This verse reminds us that true freedom comes from anchoring our identity in God rather than in opinions that constantly shift.

MORE THAN THE SCOREBOARD

Athlete Spotlight: Kerri Walsh Jennings reached the highest levels of success in her sport, earning three Olympic gold medals and establishing herself as one of beach volleyball's most dominant competitors. From the outside, her career looked flawless.

Behind the achievements, though, she has spoken honestly about the pressure to maintain perfection—not only in performance, but in leadership, discipline, and image. The expectation to always deliver became a weight she could not sustain.

That weight began to lift when her focus changed. By releasing the need to meet everyone's expectations and grounding her identity in God's truth, Kerri found freedom to compete without fear. Approval from people no longer defined her value. She learned that her worth was secure in Christ, even when mistakes were visible.

People-pleasing and perfectionism often hide beneath ambition. Many female athletes feel pressure to prove themselves, avoid failure, or meet impossible standards. Galatians 1:10 calls us to step away from that cycle. Like Kerri, you are not required to earn your value through flawless performance. You are already fully loved by God.

PATHWAY TO GROWTH

Personal Reflection: *Where do expectations feel heaviest in my athletic life? Whose approval influences my confidence the most?*

Faith in Action: Before your next practice or competition, pause and intentionally release one expectation you've been carrying. Offer it to God in a brief prayer, asking Him to help you compete from a place of trust rather than pressure. Let your focus remain on faithfulness, not perfection.

Quiet Prayer: Loving God, thank You for seeing me apart from performance and results. Help me loosen my grip on approval and rest in the truth of Your love. Teach me to compete with confidence that comes from knowing I belong to You. **Amen.**

NOTES

5

PERFECTLY DESIGNED

"For we are God's handiwork, created in Christ Jesus to do good works, which God prepared in advance for us to do."
Ephesians 2:10

Scripture Insight: Ephesians 2:10 points to a deeper truth about identity—our lives are not accidental or incomplete. Being God's handiwork means every detail of who we are was formed with intention, not oversight. This verse reminds us that purpose is woven into our design, and God can use every part of our story to accomplish good.

MORE THAN THE SCOREBOARD

Athlete Spotlight: Tamika Catchings is remembered as one of the most accomplished players in WNBA history, but her journey began far from confidence. Born with hearing loss and a speech impediment, she wore hearing aids that made her feel different and exposed. As a child, she often wished she could erase what set her apart.

Those differences became a source of shame rather than strength. Being teased for how she spoke and struggling to feel accepted made self-love feel out of reach. Tamika believed life would be easier if she could simply blend in and erase what made her unique.

Over time, her perspective began to shift. Through basketball, she developed determination, discipline, and resilience. She soon came to understand that her identity was not flawed or mistaken. What once felt like limitations became tools God used to shape her character and encourage others facing similar challenges. By choosing to see herself through God's lens rather than the world's, Tamika learned to embrace her design with confidence.

For many female athletes, the hardest battle isn't physical—it's internal. The voice that says you don't measure up can be louder than any opponent. Like Tamika, learning to value yourself doesn't require perfection. It begins with trusting that who God made you to be is enough.

PATHWAY TO GROWTH

Personal Reflection: *What part of myself do I struggle most to accept? Which strengths or qualities can I thank God for today? How can I practice healthy self-respect this week?*

Faith in Action: Choose one moment each day this week to acknowledge something God uniquely placed within you. Write it down or say it aloud as a reminder that your design has purpose. Let that awareness shape how you speak to yourself and how you step into your day.

Quiet Prayer: Heavenly God, thank You for creating me with intention and care. Help me release self-doubt and learn to see myself through Your truth. Teach me to walk with confidence in the purpose You've already prepared for my life. **Amen.**

NOTES

6

A WORK OF WONDER

"I praise you because I am fearfully and wonderfully made; your works are wonderful, I know that full well."
Psalm 139:14

Scripture Insight: Psalm 139 tells us that nothing about who we are was formed by accident. Every aspect of our strength, build, and capability was intentionally designed by God. This verse invites us to see ourselves not through comparison or criticism, but through the truth that we are created with purpose.

MORE THAN THE SCOREBOARD

Athlete Spotlight: Olympic swimmer **Missy Franklin** became known not only for her success in the pool, but for how she handled comparison and pressure off it. Standing 6'2" with broad, powerful shoulders, her body didn't match cultural expectations of femininity, and comparisons followed her closely.

Public commentary and internal pressure could have reshaped how she saw herself. Instead, Missy made a defining choice to reject those standards and ground her identity in Christ. She consistently shared that her worth was not determined by medals, media attention, or appearance. She wanted other female athletes to know that their self-worth is not tied to how they look or how others see them.

Missy's confidence flowed from understanding Psalm 139:14. What others might label as flaws or imperfections, she recognized as God-given strengths. The very traits that set her apart were the tools God used to help her excel in the pool and honor Him through her sport.

Comparison is a quiet opponent many athletes face. Body image, uniforms, and constant visibility can whisper lies that your worth is tied to appearance. God's Word speaks louder. Your value is secure because it rests in His design—not in anyone else's opinion.

PATHWAY TO GROWTH

Personal Reflection: *Where do comparisons most often creep into my thinking? What truth from Psalm 139 can I hold onto when those thoughts surface?*

Faith in Action: Choose one moment each day this week to intentionally thank God for how He designed you. Write down three strengths He has given you and revisit them when comparison arises. Let gratitude replace criticism and confidence grow from knowing your Creator makes no mistakes.

Quiet Prayer: Dear Lord, I praise You for creating me with intention and purpose. Help me release comparison and trust that I am wonderfully made according to Your design. Teach me to walk in confidence rooted in Your truth. **Amen.**

NOTES

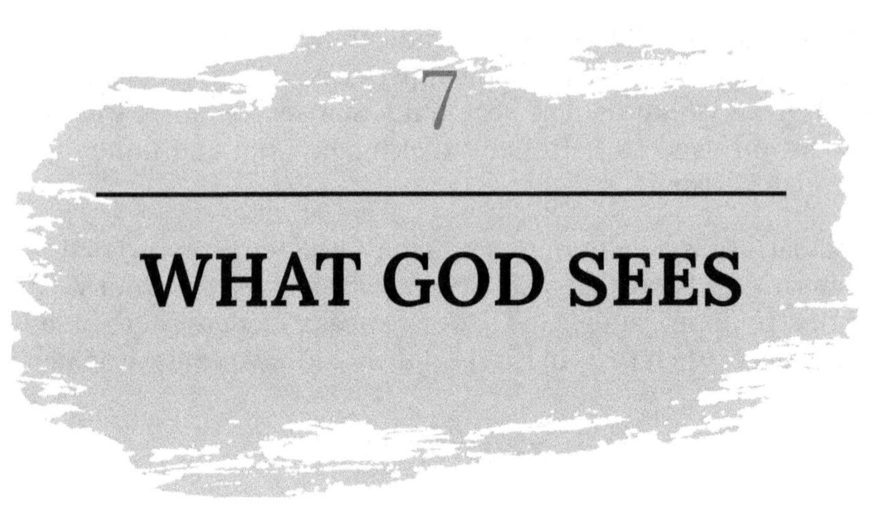

7

WHAT GOD SEES

"The Lord does not look at the things people look at. People look at the outward appearance, but the Lord looks at the heart."
1 Samuel 16:7

Scripture Insight: 1 Samuel 16:7 reveals a fundamental difference between human judgment and God's perspective. While people are drawn to what is visible and impressive, God evaluates what cannot be seen at first glance. This verse reminds us that character, faith, and the condition of the heart matter far more than outward appearance to Him.

MORE THAN THE SCOREBOARD

Athlete Spotlight: Cheerleading is often misunderstood, reduced to assumptions about appearance rather than recognized for the strength, discipline, and leadership it requires. **Reece Weaver**, a professional cheerleader and outspoken Christian, has experienced those misconceptions firsthand.

Throughout her career, she has faced labels placed on cheerleaders—judgments about worth, dismissive attitudes toward the sport, and pressure to fit a narrow image. Rather than allowing those opinions to shape her identity, Reece has chosen to speak openly about rejecting stereotypes and grounding her confidence in what God says about her.

Her response reflects the truth of 1 Samuel 16:7. While others focus on titles, uniforms, or appearances, Reece points attention back to the heart. She reminds athletes that identity is not determined by how the world categorizes you, but by the value God has already placed within you.

Stereotypes can weigh heavily on female athletes. You may have been told you are "too much," "not enough," or easily dismissed by a label that fails to capture who you truly are. God does not see those labels. He sees your heart, your faith, and the purpose He designed you for. When you choose to live from His perspective, no stereotype can limit what He is calling you to become.

PATHWAY TO GROWTH

Personal Reflection: *What labels have followed me in my sport? What would change if I prioritized God's perspective over others' opinions?*

Faith in Action: Take one label you've internalized and write it down. Then replace it with a truth rooted in Scripture, such as "God looks at my heart" or "I am known and valued by Him." Return to that truth whenever stereotypes try to shape how you see yourself.

Quiet Prayer: Dear Father, thank You for seeing beyond appearances and knowing my heart completely. Help me release the labels placed on me by others and live confidently in the truth of who You say I am. Teach me to value Your perspective above all else. **Amen.**

NOTES

8

WHERE TO LOOK

"Let us fix our eyes on Jesus, the author and perfecter of our faith."
Hebrews 12:2

Scripture Insight: Hebrews 12:2 redirects our attention away from shifting distractions and toward a steady source of truth. Fixing our eyes on Jesus means choosing focus intentionally, even when other voices compete for attention. This verse reminds us that clarity, confidence, and endurance grow when Christ, not culture, sets the direction of our gaze.

MORE THAN THE SCOREBOARD

Athlete Spotlight: Coco Gauff stepped onto one of tennis's biggest stages at a remarkably young age, and her life changed almost overnight. With global attention came constant evaluation of her performance, her appearance, and even her personality.

Praise followed wins, while criticism surfaced after losses. Social media amplified everything, creating a stream of comparisons and opinions that began to wear on her confidence. Coco later shared that scrolling through comments and highlight reels affected how she viewed herself.

Rather than letting online voices shape her identity, Coco made a deliberate choice to step back. By limiting social media and guarding her focus, she shifted her attention to what truly grounded her—her faith and the joy of competing with purpose. Her confidence grew not from maintaining an online image, but from fixing her eyes on Christ, whose view of her never changes.

For many female athletes, comparison feels unavoidable in a screen-driven world. Constant exposure to curated images and performances can quietly erode confidence. When focus returns to Christ, however, the noise begins to fade. Self-worth no longer rises and falls with likes or comments, because it is anchored in the truth of who He is and how He sees you.

PATHWAY TO GROWTH

Personal Reflection: *How does social media influence the way I view myself as an athlete? Where am I most tempted to compare my athletic journey to someone else's?*

Faith in Action: Choose one intentional adjustment to your media habits this week. It might be setting a time limit, muting accounts that trigger comparison, or replacing a scroll with a brief moment of prayer. Each time comparison surfaces, pause and redirect your focus back to the truth of Hebrews 12:2.

Quiet Prayer: Dear God, thank You for reminding me where true worth is found. Help me guard my heart from comparison and keep my focus centered on You. Shape my confidence through Your truth, not the noise around me. **Amen.**

NOTES

CHAPTER 3: CHARACTER THAT HONORS & RESPECTS

9

WHEN NO ONE'S WATCHING

"The integrity of the upright guides them, but the unfaithful are destroyed by their duplicity."
Proverbs 11:3

Scripture Insight: Proverbs 11:3 points to integrity as the force that directs the lives of those who walk uprightly. Integrity is not something that appears only in public moments. It shapes decisions made in private, when effort, honesty, and discipline are tested without recognition. This verse reminds us that character guides us long before results ever speak for us.

MORE THAN THE SCOREBOARD

Athlete Spotlight: In rodeo, most people see only the final run, but the foundation is built long before the crowd arrives. Barrel racer **Taylor Decker** understands that reality well. Her sport requires early mornings, patient training, and quiet repetition that no audience celebrates.

Taylor has spoken openly about her faith and how it shapes the way she approaches competition. For her, success is not measured only by results but by honoring Christ in how she treats teammates, competitors, animals, and the people working behind the scenes.

Training with integrity means she prepares the same way whether eyes are on her or not. From caring for her horse to practicing patterns and handling long travel days, she chooses consistency, humility, and respect over shortcuts or self-promotion.

Taylor's example reflects Proverbs 11:3. Integrity becomes the guide when no one is watching, and character becomes the victory that lasts longer than any buckle or arena spotlight.

PATHWAY TO GROWTH

Personal Reflection: *When I train or compete without supervision, do my choices reflect integrity? Where am I tempted to take shortcuts instead of doing what is right? What would it look like to let my character lead this week?*

Faith in Action: Identify one moment this week where integrity will require extra effort or honesty. Commit to that choice in advance. Small decisions made consistently build strength that carries into competition and life beyond sport.

Quiet Prayer: Dear Lord, thank You for showing me that integrity is a guide I can trust. Help me choose honesty, effort, and respect in every situation. Teach me to value character over recognition and to walk in truth, even when no one is watching. **Amen.**

NOTES

10

RESPECT WITHOUT EXCEPTION

"Show proper respect to everyone, love the family of believers, fear God, honor the emperor."
1 Peter 2:17

Scripture Insight: 1 Peter 2:17 calls believers to live with intentional honor toward everyone they encounter. Respect is not selective or situational. It shapes how we speak, respond, and compete, especially in moments of tension or disagreement. This verse reminds us that honoring others reflects reverence for God Himself.

MORE THAN THE SCOREBOARD

Athlete Spotlight: Brittany Lincicome has earned a reputation on the LPGA Tour that extends beyond her powerful play. As a two-time major champion, she is widely respected not only for her success, but for how she treats the people around her.

Rather than letting achievement elevate her above others, Brittany has consistently chosen humility and kindness. She is known for encouraging younger players, acknowledging competitors, and taking time with fans even after demanding rounds. Her actions show that respect is expressed through consistent choices, not public recognition.

Her example reflects the heart of 1 Peter 2:17. Wins may fade from memory, but character leaves a lasting mark. Brittany demonstrates that respect is not weakness. It is strength rooted in Christ, shown through dignity, encouragement, and honor in every interaction.

Respect shapes how athletes are remembered. The way you treat officials, opponents, teammates, and supporters speaks louder than statistics. When respect guides your conduct, your witness carries weight and brings honor to God through sport.

PATHWAY TO GROWTH

Personal Reflection: *Do I show the same level of respect to officials and opponents as I do to teammates? In what situations is it hardest for me to respond with honor? How can respect shape my attitude this week?*

Faith in Action: Plan one intentional act of respect before your next competition. It might be offering gratitude to an official, acknowledging an opponent's effort, or encouraging a teammate who is struggling. Let respect become a visible expression of your faith.

Quiet Prayer: Gracious Father, thank You for calling me to honor others as You do. Help me compete with humility, integrity, and respect in every situation. May my actions reflect Your character more clearly than any result or recognition. **Amen.**

NOTES

11

IN WORD & DEED

"And whatever you do, whether in word or deed, do it all in the name of the Lord Jesus, giving thanks to God the Father through him."

Colossians 3:17

Scripture Insight: Colossians 3:17 calls believers to live with intentional purpose in every action and every word. Doing something in Jesus' name means approaching each moment with gratitude, respect, and awareness of God's presence. This includes preparation, practice, and performance, turning ordinary effort into an act of worship.

MORE THAN THE SCOREBOARD

Athlete Spotlight: Simone Biles is often recognized for her unmatched achievements, including seven Olympic medals and dozens of world titles. Yet what truly sets her apart is not only what she has accomplished, but how she approaches her sport.

In training, Simone is known for her focus and discipline. She treats every repetition with intention, supports those around her, and respects the process behind excellence. She has spoken openly about her faith, acknowledging her abilities as gifts from God and choosing to compete with gratitude rather than for applause.

That perspective became clear to the world during the 2021 Tokyo Olympics when Simone stepped away from several events to protect her mental health. While many struggled to understand her decision, it reflected something deeper. She chose to honor what God values most, placing her well being above medals and scores. Through that choice, she reminded others that faith is lived out not only in victories, but in wise and reverent decisions.

Simone's example shows that true greatness is shaped by reverence. Training with integrity, competing with gratitude, and honoring God through every effort reflects a life lived fully in His name.

PATHWAY TO GROWTH

Personal Reflection: *Do I approach training with intention and gratitude, or simply try to get through it? What would change if I treated each repetition as an offering to God?*

Faith in Action: Choose one part of your routine this week to approach with deeper focus and thankfulness. It might be warm ups, recovery, or conditioning. Pause briefly before you begin and offer that effort to God, committing to stay present and intentional throughout.

Quiet Prayer: Almighty God, thank You for the abilities and opportunities You have placed in my life. Teach me to honor You in every word and every action. May my effort, attitude, and discipline reflect gratitude and reverence for all You have given me. **Amen.**

NOTES

12

INTEGRITY ALWAYS WINS

"Whoever walks in integrity walks securely, but whoever takes crooked paths will be found out."
Proverbs 10:9

Scripture Insight: Proverbs 10:9 connects integrity with stability and peace. Living with honesty and consistency creates a sense of security that does not depend on results or recognition. This verse reminds athletes that while records change and awards fade, character provides a foundation that lasts.

MORE THAN THE SCOREBOARD

Athlete Spotlight: Julie Chu competed at the highest level as a four time Olympian for Team USA Hockey. While she earned medals and respect on the ice, those around her often speak first about her integrity rather than her statistics.

After difficult Olympic losses, Julie was known for showing genuine respect to opponents, including moments where she comforted rival players with sincerity. Her response to disappointment revealed what mattered most to her. Relationships, humility, and honor carried greater weight than the final score.

Julie's career reflects the truth of Proverbs 10:9. Her confidence did not rise and fall with wins or losses because it was rooted in character. Teammates, coaches, and even competitors consistently describe her as one of the most respected players in the sport. Her legacy was shaped by how she carried herself, not by the numbers on a scoresheet.

For every athlete, integrity offers a steadier source of confidence than comparison or clout. Results will shift over time, but character grounded in faith continues to speak long after competition ends.

PATHWAY TO GROWTH

Personal Reflection: *What am I prioritizing most right now, performance or character? How do I respond to teammates and opponents when outcomes do not go my way? Where is God inviting me to walk with greater integrity?*

Faith in Action: Choose one moment this week to place character above results. It might mean acknowledging a teammate's success, admitting a mistake, or showing respect after a tough loss. Let your actions reflect that integrity matters more than statistics.

Quiet Prayer: Heavenly Father, thank You for showing me that integrity leads to true security. Help me value character above recognition and treat others with honesty and respect. Teach me to walk confidently in Your truth, knowing that integrity honors You. **Amen.**

NOTES

CHAPTER 4: A HUMBLE & THANKFUL HEART

13

CROWNED IN HUMILITY

"All of you, clothe yourselves with humility toward one another, because, 'God opposes the proud but shows favor to the humble.'"
1 Peter 5:5

Scripture Insight: 1 Peter 5:5 presents humility as something we actively choose to wear. Just as an athlete puts on a uniform before stepping into competition, humility should be visible in attitude, response, and conduct. This verse reminds us that talent is not diminished by humility, but properly framed when we remember it is a gift from God rather than a source of pride.

MORE THAN THE SCOREBOARD

Athlete Spotlight: Shawn Johnson East understands the pressure that comes with high expectations. During the 2008 Beijing Olympics, many anticipated she would dominate every event. Instead, her results included three silver medals and one gold, outcomes that could have easily led to disappointment or comparison.

Rather than focusing on what she did not win, Shawn chose humility. She celebrated her teammates, openly praised Nastia Liukin's success, and expressed gratitude for being part of a strong team. Her response showed that humility means honoring others even when the spotlight shifts away from you.

That mindset continued beyond the competition floor. Shawn has spoken honestly about struggles with identity and body image, emphasizing that medals do not determine worth. Today, she uses her platform to encourage and mentor others, choosing transparency over self-promotion. Her story reflects the heart of 1 Peter 5:5 by showing that humility reveals character and points others toward Christ.

Humility does not hide talent. It places it in the right context. When humility shapes how you compete and respond, your witness becomes stronger than any result.

PATHWAY TO GROWTH

Personal Reflection: *How can I practice humility in the way I treat teammates or opponents? Do I find it difficult to celebrate others when they succeed? Where do I need to remember that my abilities are gifts rather than my identity?*

Faith in Action: Look for one opportunity this week to shift attention away from yourself. Acknowledge a teammate's effort, celebrate an opponent's success, or express gratitude instead of seeking recognition. Let humility be as noticeable as the uniform you wear.

Quiet Prayer: Lord Jesus, thank You for showing me that humility is a strength that honors You. Help me wear humility in my actions, my words, and my responses. Teach me to use every gift You have given me to point back to You. **Amen.**

NOTES

14

WALK HUMBLY WITH GOD

"He has shown you, O mortal, what is good. And what does the Lord require of you? To act justly and to love mercy and to walk humbly with your God."
Micah 6:8

Scripture Insight: Micah 6:8 shifts the focus away from performance and recognition and places it on daily faithfulness. God does not ask for perfection or applause driven success. He calls His people to live with fairness, extend mercy, and walk closely with Him in humility. This verse reminds us that honoring God happens through consistent character, not through spotlight moments.

MORE THAN THE SCOREBOARD

Athlete Spotlight: Natasha Foutz became known in softball not for chasing recognition, but for consistent humble character and steady leadership. While she competed at a high level, her influence grew through how she poured into teammates and carried her faith into competitive spaces.

Natasha often speaks about resisting the pressure to make sport about personal achievement. Instead, she chose to invest in others, mentor younger athletes, and view competition as a way to honor Christ.

Her posture in practices, dugouts, and training environments showed humility in action. Natasha redirected praise to God, treated opponents with respect, and embraced influence without demanding attention.

Her example reflects Micah 6:8. She demonstrates that true greatness is not built on spotlight moments, but on daily obedience and character shaped by faith. Walking humbly with God is what leads to lasting victory.

PATHWAY TO GROWTH

Personal Reflection: *Where am I tempted to seek attention or credit in my sport? What does walking humbly with God look like during practice and competition? How can I intentionally celebrate others this week?*

Faith in Action: Look for one opportunity this week to place others first. Encourage a teammate, express gratitude to a coach, or show respect to an opponent. Choose humility as a visible reflection of your faith and confidence in Christ.

Quiet Prayer: Jesus, thank You for showing me that humility brings freedom and strength. Help me walk closely with You, act with integrity, and place others above myself. Teach me to carry a humble heart in every practice, competition, and conversation. **Amen.**

NOTES

15

THANKFUL IN THE WAVES

"Give thanks in all circumstances; for this is God's will for you in Christ Jesus."
1 Thessalonians 5:18

Scripture Insight: 1 Thessalonians 5:18 invites believers to practice gratitude even when circumstances feel heavy or uncertain. Giving thanks does not deny pain or loss. Instead, it reflects trust that God is present and purposeful in every season. Gratitude becomes a steady anchor when emotions and outcomes feel unpredictable.

MORE THAN THE SCOREBOARD

Athlete Spotlight: Bethany Hamilton faced a life-altering moment at a young age when a shark attack during a surfing session in Hawaii cost her an arm and nearly her life. The incident instantly changed her future and challenged everything she knew about her sport.

Rather than walking away from the ocean, Bethany chose to return. Within weeks she was back in the water, and within a short time she was competing again at elite levels. Her determination reflected deep resilience rooted in faith, not fear.

What stands out most in Bethany's journey is her posture of gratitude. She has consistently expressed thankfulness, not for the trauma itself, but for how God has used her story. She focuses on what remains possible rather than what was lost, choosing trust and gratitude over bitterness.

Her life reflects the truth of 1 Thessalonians 5:18. Hard seasons do not define an athlete, but response does. Gratitude shifts perspective from loss to purpose and from pain to hope grounded in Christ.

PATHWAY TO GROWTH

Personal **Reflection:** *What challenge am I facing where gratitude feels difficult? What is one thing I can thank God for today, even in the middle of uncertainty?*

Faith in Action: Set aside a few minutes this week to write down three things you are grateful for during a challenging season. Bring those items to God in prayer. Ask Him to help you recognize where He is working, even when progress feels slow.

Quiet Prayer: Dear God, thank You for remaining faithful in every circumstance. Help me choose gratitude when my situation feels overwhelming. Teach me to trust Your purpose and to let thankfulness shape my attitude, even when the path ahead is unclear. **Amen.**

NOTES

16

SEEK FIRST HIS KINGDOM

"But seek first his kingdom and his righteousness, and all these things will be given to you as well."
Matthew 6:33

Scripture Insight: Matthew 6:33 sets a clear priority for how Christians are called to live. Seeking God's Kingdom first means placing His values above recognition, success, or outcomes. When God is given first place, He promises to provide what truly lasts: peace, identity, and purpose that do not depend on performance.

MORE THAN THE SCOREBOARD

Athlete Spotlight: Sydney McLaughlin-Levrone stepped into global attention early in her career after qualifying for the U.S. Olympic team and later redefining what was possible in the 400 meter hurdles. Records fell, headlines followed, and the spotlight grew brighter with every race.

Rather than letting fame become the goal, Sydney consistently chose a different focus. She has spoken openly about placing her faith above accolades and redirecting praise back to Christ. After record breaking performances, she has reminded the world that achievements fade, but God's glory remains.

Her life reflects the truth of Matthew 6:33. Whether celebrated or scrutinized, Sydney keeps her priorities aligned with God's Kingdom. She shows that success does not require chasing attention, and that confidence grows when identity is rooted in Christ rather than public approval.

For female athletes, her example offers clarity. Popularity, trophies, and applause shift over time. Seeking God first creates a foundation that does not move, no matter the outcome.

PATHWAY TO GROWTH

Personal Reflection: *Where am I tempted to seek recognition or approval through my sport? What would it look like for me to put God's Kingdom first in my training and competition? How can my attitude reflect trust in His plan?*

Faith in Action: After your next practice, workout, or competition, pause and intentionally redirect the focus. Thank God in prayer, acknowledge a teammate, or give credit away instead of taking it. These small choices train your heart to seek God's Kingdom above recognition.

Quiet Prayer: Dear Father, thank You for reminding me where true success is found. Help me place Your Kingdom above results, attention, and applause. Teach me to use my gifts with humility and trust, knowing Your plans are greater than anything the world offers. **Amen.**

NOTES

SECTION II: THE PATH TO GROWTH

(WEEKS 17 - 35)

Greatness is built through consistent effort, intentional discipline, and perseverance anchored in faith. This section invites female athletes to lean into the daily process, developing patience, mental toughness, and focus that sustain growth over time. Rather than avoiding challenges, these devotions encourage you to meet adversity with resilience and a Christ-centered perspective.

Through real stories and purposeful training lessons, you will learn how to stay committed when progress feels slow and pressure feels heavy. The focus extends beyond improving performance. It is about shaping character, strengthening resolve, and deepening spiritual maturity so that growth happens both on the field and within the heart.

CHAPTER 5: DISCIPLINE THAT FUELS GROWTH

17

TRAINING FOR THE CROWN

"Everyone who competes in the games goes into strict training. They do it to get a crown that will not last, but we do it to get a crown that will last forever."
1 Corinthians 9:25

Scripture Insight: In 1 Corinthians 9:25, Paul highlights the difference between fleeting prizes and the eternal reward found in Christ. Medals lose their shine, but spiritual discipline endures. When athletes entrust their routines and goals to God, training becomes an act of worship that builds something time cannot touch.

MORE THAN THE SCOREBOARD

Athlete Spotlight: Consistency often separates good athletes from great ones. **Gabrielle Reece** became widely known for her success on the volleyball court, but what sustained her over time was her commitment to disciplined daily habits.

From the earliest stages of her career, training was approached with intention. Strength work, recovery, nutrition, and rest were treated as non-negotiables, allowing her to remain competitive year after year.

Her discipline also extended beyond competition. Gabrielle prioritized faith, family, and personal health, recognizing that honoring God involved more than performance alone.

For her, success was not defined by trophies but by stewarding her gifts with integrity. Her example shows that daily habits can become acts of worship, shaping character and revealing the priorities of the heart.

PATHWAY TO GROWTH

Personal Reflection: *What patterns shape my days right now? Which habit could better reflect my commitment to God if I strengthened it? How might ordinary routines become opportunities to honor Him with intention?*

Faith in Action: Choose one simple practice to focus on this week. It might be pausing to pray before training, expressing gratitude during a workout, or speaking encouragement to a teammate. Commit to practicing it consistently and view that discipline as an act of worship offered to God.

Quiet Prayer: Dear Lord, thank You for the way You use daily choices to shape my heart and character. I am grateful for the opportunity to honor You through discipline and consistency. Help me build routines that reflect my faith and glorify You, not only in visible moments but in the quiet work of each day. **Amen.**

NOTES

18

HEAVENLY MINDED DISCIPLINE

"Set your minds on things above, not on earthly things."
Colossians 3:2

Scripture Insight: Colossians 3:2 directs believers to set their minds on what is eternal rather than chasing temporary recognition. In athletics, this reorders motivation at its core. Training without a higher purpose can become exhausting, even when results look impressive. But when the mind is anchored in Christ, discipline gains meaning, direction, and spiritual weight. Ordinary routines become expressions of devotion that shape both character and faith.

MORE THAN THE SCOREBOARD

Athlete Spotlight: Sustaining excellence over decades is rare, and **Dara Torres** distinguished herself not only through accomplishments, but through unwavering commitment to the process. Competing in five Olympic Games across a 24-year span, she returned to elite competition repeatedly with remarkable clarity of purpose.

Her journey included injuries, long recoveries, and the transition into motherhood. Yet she maintained disciplined habits and refused to let distractions or assumptions define her limits. At 41, she returned to the Olympic stage, challenging expectations about age and possibility through focused preparation and relentless consistency.

What carried her forward was not talent alone, but a mindset anchored when circumstances shifted. Her example invites athletes to evaluate where their attention rests. Is it pulled toward pressure and comparison, or grounded in honoring God through steady obedience? When faith leads, even ordinary training carries eternal significance.

PATHWAY TO GROWTH

Personal Reflection: *Where does my attention tend to drift most easily? What distractions weaken my consistency or motivation? How can I bring greater intentionality into my training this week?*

Faith in Action: Identify one habit that has become inconsistent or rushed. Recommit to it with purpose, beginning each session by mentally offering your effort to God. Let focus guide your discipline, not emotion or circumstance.

Quiet Prayer: Lord, help me lift my thoughts above temporary outcomes and fix them on what truly matters. Align my focus with Your truth so my discipline is shaped by faith, not pressure. May my training reflect a heart that seeks to honor You in every effort. **Amen.**

NOTES

19

THE OBEDIENT HEART

"Let us fix our eyes on Jesus, the author and perfecter of our faith." "Anyone who loves me will obey my teaching. My Father will love them, and we will come to them and make our home with them."
John 14:23

Scripture Insight: John 14:23 reveals that obedience is not rooted in obligation but in relationship. God invites us to follow His ways because we love Him, not because we are trying to earn His favor. In an athlete's life, obedience shows up in everyday moments that often go unnoticed. It shapes how you respond to instruction, manage rest, speak to others, and make choices when emotions or plans shift. Choosing God's direction in those moments reflects trust, humility, and a heart that desires to honor Him.

MORE THAN THE SCOREBOARD

Athlete Spotlight: In disciplines like cheer and dance, success depends on repetition, unity, and precision, yet character is revealed long before competition day. **Claire Wolford** demonstrates how a sincere love for Christ can guide both performance and perspective. Her commitment extends beyond physical preparation and into how she approaches each part of her routine.

She builds her habits around faith by starting practices with prayer, offering encouragement when teammates struggle, and respecting leadership even when adjustments are difficult. Away from the gym, she remains intentional with rest, personal conduct, and the way she presents herself publicly. Rather than chasing attention or approval, her choices reflect a desire to stay aligned with God's Word.

What stands out most is not a single routine, but the consistency of her obedience. Her example reminds athletes that faithfulness is formed through daily decisions. When Scripture directs your habits, your ability becomes a witness.

Training the body matters, yet training the heart through obedience is what gives lasting purpose to your sport.

PATHWAY TO GROWTH

Personal Reflection: *Are my choices guided by Christ even when no one sees them? Where do I feel resistance when God calls me to obey? How can love for God shape my decisions this week?*

Faith in Action: Select one area where obedience has felt inconsistent, such as your attitude, online presence, or response to authority. Intentionally choose God's way in that space each day and observe how consistency strengthens both character and focus.

Quiet Prayer: Lord, thank You for inviting mc into a life shaped by love and obedience. Align my heart with Your truth so my actions reflect my faith. Help me honor You through the choices I make in training, competition, and everyday lifc. **Amen.**

NOTES

20

ANCHORED IN PRAYER

"Devote yourselves to prayer, being watchful and thankful."
Colossians 4:2

Scripture Insight: Colossians 4:2 urges believers to commit themselves fully to prayer, treating it as a steady practice rather than a last resort. Devotion implies intention, consistency, and priority. For athletes, prayer becomes the place where focus is reset and gratitude is formed before outcomes are known. When prayer is woven into daily rhythms, it strengthens awareness of God's presence and keeps the heart steady no matter what the scoreboard shows.

MORE THAN THE SCOREBOARD

Athlete Spotlight: Before **Lauren Daigle** became a well-known Christian singer and songwriter, she spent her college years competing on LSU's beach volleyball team. Teammates recall that before practices and matches she often prayed for clarity and peace, asking God to steady her heart and align her focus. That rhythm helped her compete with freedom rather than fear.

As her athletic path shifted toward music, that same discipline of prayer carried into her calling. Lauren often describes prayer as the center of her life, a place where she surrenders outcomes and asks God to lead. Whether preparing for a performance or stepping into new opportunities, prayer keeps her identity rooted in Christ instead of public approval.

Her example reflects the message of Colossians 4:2. Prayer is not treated as a last-minute plea when circumstances feel heavy, but as a consistent practice of thanksgiving and trust that shapes both mindset and purpose.

Her journey reminds athletes that prayer belongs in the middle of preparation, competition, and pressure. When prayer leads, the heart stays anchored and purpose becomes clearer than the scoreboard or the noise surrounding it.

PATHWAY TO GROWTH

Personal Reflection: *How consistently do I bring prayer into my sport? Do I turn to God only under pressure or invite Him into the process every day? Where can prayer become a more natural part of my routine?*

Faith in Action: Choose one consistent moment to pray this week, such as before training, during warmups, or after competition. Keep it simple and intentional, thanking God for the opportunity to compete and asking Him to guide your focus and attitude.

Quiet Prayer: My God, thank You for the gift of prayer that anchors my heart and mind. Help me remain faithful in seeking You through every practice and competition. Teach me to rely on Your presence more than outcomes so my sport continually reflects Your grace. **Amen.**

NOTES

CHAPTER 6: STRONG MIND TO STRONG FINISH

21

POWER PERFECT IN WEAKNESS

"But he said to me, 'My grace is sufficient for you, for my power is made perfect in weakness.' Therefore I will boast all the more gladly about my weaknesses, so that Christ's power may rest on me."

2 Corinthians 12:9

Scripture Insight: In 2 Corinthians 12:9, God reframes weakness as a place where His power is most clearly displayed. Rather than requiring perfection, He invites surrender, showing that dependence on His grace creates space for strength beyond our own. When limitations are acknowledged instead of hidden, God's presence becomes unmistakable.

MORE THAN THE SCOREBOARD

Athlete Spotlight: Resilience in sport is often forged through hardship, not ease. **Lindsey Vonn** built one of the most remarkable careers in alpine skiing while repeatedly facing physical adversity. As one of the most accomplished skiers in history, she endured injuries that would have ended many careers, including torn ligaments, concussions, fractures, and multiple surgeries.

Each setback required more than physical recovery. Lindsey chose to rise again, refusing to let pain or disappointment determine her future, and her journey was marked by composure and humility rather than self-promotion.

She often shared that skiing was not solely about winning, but about testing limits and navigating obstacles with strength and grace. Falling did not disqualify her. Returning with resolve did.

Her story reframes grit for athletes facing injury, loss, doubt, or criticism: strength is not proven by avoiding failure, but by persevering with grace. When determination is paired with reliance on God's sustaining power, weakness becomes a place where His strength is revealed. That is grit anchored in faith.

PATHWAY TO GROWTH

Personal Reflection: *Where is resilience being tested in my sport right now? What would it look like to depend on God's grace rather than forcing my own strength? Can I recall a moment when God used a weakness to shape something meaningful in me?*

Faith in Action: Choose one area where you feel stretched or limited, whether physical, mental, or spiritual. Write it down and bring it to God each day this week. Ask Him to meet you there and guide how you train and compete.

Quiet Prayer: God, thank You for reminding me that lasting strength comes from You. I'm grateful for Your grace in moments of struggle. Teach me to rise with perseverance, respond with humility, and trust Your power to carry me through challenges. **Amen.**

NOTES

22

UNBREAKABLE FAITH

"We are hard pressed on every side, but not crushed; perplexed, but not in despair; persecuted, but not abandoned; struck down, but not destroyed."
2 Corinthians 4:8–9

Scripture Insight: In 2 Corinthians 4:8–9, Paul acknowledges the reality of pressure, confusion, and hardship without sugarcoating the struggle. Faith does not remove adversity, but it anchors us so we are not overwhelmed or defeated by it. Even when circumstances feel heavy and strength feels limited, God's presence remains constant and sustaining.

MORE THAN THE SCOREBOARD

Athlete Spotlight: Tatyana McFadden, a decorated Paralympian and distance racing champion, shows how faith can steady the heart when adversity presses from all sides. Born with spina bifida and abandoned in a Russian orphanage, she learned to move using only her arms before being adopted into the United States.

When she entered wheelchair racing, surgeries, eligibility disputes, and long stretches of rehabilitation tested her patience and confidence. Training demanded endurance that reached beyond physical strength.

Through those seasons, Tatyana credited God for her story, her opportunities, and the resilience to continue. Paralympic medals and major marathon titles became evidence of quiet persistence formed through faith rather than ease.

Her journey reflects 2 Corinthians 4:8–9. Though pressed by hardship, she was not crushed. Unbreakable faith does not avoid difficulty. It endures through it.

PATHWAY TO GROWTH

Personal Reflection: *Where does pressure feel heaviest in my sport right now? What would change if I relied on God's strength instead of pushing only through my own effort? How can faith reshape the way I respond to setbacks or disappointment?*

Faith in Action: When difficulty arises this week, pause and intentionally speak truth over the moment. Remind yourself that pressure does not equal defeat and that your strength is rooted in Christ. Write a Scripture or affirmation of faith and keep it nearby as a steady reminder during training or competition.

Quiet Prayer: Gracious God, thank You for the strength You place within me through Your Spirit. I am grateful that no challenge can overpower the hope You give. Help me face adversity with confidence, trust Your presence in every moment, and remember that in You I am never abandoned. **Amen.**

NOTES

23

ALL IN FOR CHRIST

"Commit to the Lord whatever you do, and he will establish your plans."
Proverbs 16:3

Scripture Insight: Proverbs 16:3 invites us to move beyond partial faith and into full surrender. When our preparation, ambition, and effort are placed in God's care, He brings clarity and direction that go deeper than results alone. Trusting Him with the work we do daily allows our discipline to shape both our performance and our hearts.

MORE THAN THE SCOREBOARD

Athlete Spotlight: Cheyenne Knight has built her career on the LPGA Tour through disciplined preparation and a deeper commitment to her faith. Hours of practice on ball-striking, short game, and course management are matched with strength work that supports consistency throughout long tournament weeks. Yet Cheyenne has shared that the most important part of her preparation is spiritual. Scripture and prayer travel with her from event to event, helping her compete with clarity and purpose rather than anxiety.

That perspective reflects the heart of Proverbs 16:3. Cheyenne entrusts her plans to the Lord rather than trying to control every outcome. After earning her first LPGA victory, she publicly thanked God for the opportunity and acknowledged that her identity is rooted in Christ, not in rankings or trophies.

When tournaments have been disappointing, she has spoken about placing results in God's hands and allowing Him to shape her path forward. That steady confidence frees her to work hard without letting pressure dictate her worth or her peace.

Cheyenne models what it looks like to be fully committed to Christ in sport. Discipline honors God, but surrender glorifies Him. When preparation and ambition are entrusted to the Lord, He brings a steadiness and joy that performance alone cannot produce.

PATHWAY TO GROWTH

Personal Reflection: *Which area of your training or competition feels hardest to release? What might change if you trusted God with that part of your routine?*

Faith in Action: Identify one habit you often rush or overlook, such as recovery, preparation, or mental focus. This week, pause before beginning and offer that moment to God. Let consistency become an act of faith, not just discipline.

Quiet Prayer: Lord, thank You for the opportunity to honor You through my sport. Help me place my effort, goals, and cxpcctations in Your care each day. Teach me to trust You with the work I put in and the outcome that follows. **Amen.**

NOTES

CHAPTER 7: FROM RESILIENCE TO RECOVERY

24

GLORY IN THE STRUGGLE

"*We also glory in our sufferings, because we know that suffering produces perseverance; perseverance, character; and character, hope.*"
Romans 5:3–4

Scripture Insight: Romans 5:3–4 reframes hardship as a process rather than a setback. Pressure and pain do not appear randomly in our lives; they work together to build endurance, refine character, and anchor hope. When viewed through faith, even difficult seasons can become instruments God uses to strengthen what lasts.

MORE THAN THE SCOREBOARD

Athlete Spotlight: Kayla Montgomery's story in distance running is a striking picture of perseverance formed through hardship. Diagnosed with multiple sclerosis as a teenager, she learned that as her body heated during races, she would gradually lose sensation in her legs. What felt like a closed door to most became her platform to endure through faith.

Instead of walking away, Kayla continued training and competing with purpose. Coaches would prepare to physically catch her at the finish because her legs often collapsed immediately after crossing the line. Every race demanded courage. Every finish required resilience of mind, body, and spirit.

What set Kayla apart was not only her performance, but her perspective. She chose to view adversity as shaping, not defeating. Prayer, Scripture, and community helped her remain grounded when setbacks and fear crept in. Over time, her story inspired countless athletes who recognized that victory is not always measured in medals, but in staying the course when trials press in.

Kayla's experience reflects the truth of Romans 5:3–4. Suffering produced perseverance, perseverance formed character, and character anchored a hope that pointed beyond the track to the God who restores and strengthens His people in the struggle.

PATHWAY TO GROWTH

Personal Reflection: *Which challenge in your athletic career as stretched you the most? How might perseverance reshape that experience rather than defeat you? Where can you see character being formed through difficulty?*

Faith in Action: Choose one struggle you are currently facing and write it down. Each day this week, pray through Romans 5:3–4, asking God to develop perseverance and strengthen your character as you wait with hope.

Quiet Prayer: Heavenly Father, thank You for working even in seasons of hardship. Give me the strength to endure and the faith to trust that You are shaping something good within me. Help my hope remain steady as You continue Your work. **Amen.**

NOTES

25

STRENGTH TO RISE AGAIN

"But those who hope in the Lord will renew their strength. They will soar on wings like eagles; they will run and not grow weary, they will walk and not be faint."
Isaiah 40:31

Scripture Insight: Isaiah 40:31 speaks to a kind of strength that is restored rather than forced. Biblical hope is not passive or uncertain; it is active trust placed in God while effort continues. Waiting on the Lord often looks like consistent preparation, honest recovery, and the courage to begin again after disappointment, all while anchoring identity in Christ rather than performance or recognition.

MORE THAN THE SCOREBOARD

Athlete Spotlight: Simone Manuel's career shows that strength can be renewed rather than forced. After becoming the first Black woman to win individual Olympic gold in swimming, she faced intense expectations and later developed overtraining syndrome, which forced her to step away from competition for a season.

Instead of pushing through burnout, she chose honest rest and recovery, trusting that rebuilding slowly still mattered. During that time, Simone leaned on prayer and Scripture to reshape her identity and remind herself that God, not medals, defines her worth.

When she returned to competition, her strength was different, marked by patience, steadiness, and peace rooted in Christ rather than pressure. Simone models the truth of Isaiah 40:31, showing that those who place their hope in the Lord find renewed strength to rise again.

Her story reminds female athletes that renewal is often slow, but God's restoring work is never wasted.

PATHWAY TO GROWTH

Personal Reflection: *Where do you most need God to restore your strength right now? What would it look like to trust Him when motivation feels low? Which setback could become part of your growth story?*

Faith in Action: Choose one moment this week when training feels heavy or progress feels slow. Pause briefly, acknowledge God's presence, and then take the next faithful step. Finish the set, complete the recovery work, or show up again tomorrow, trusting Him to renew your strength over time.

Quiet Prayer: Dear Jesus, thank You for sustaining me when my energy fades and my confidence wavers. Help me trust You through rebuilding seasons and remain faithful in the process. Restore my strength in Your timing so my journey reflects Your purpose. **Amen.**

NOTES

26

BEYOND THE SURFACE

"The Lord does not look at the things people look at. People look at the outward appearance, but the Lord looks at the heart."
1 Samuel 16:7

Scripture Insight: In 1 Samuel 16:7, God makes it clear that His measure of a person goes far deeper than what is visible. While people are drawn to appearance, performance, and recognition, the Lord examines the heart. When God evaluates the heart, integrity carries more weight than image, and obedience matters more than applause. Living from the inside out allows Him to shape not only how you play, but who you are becoming.

MORE THAN THE SCOREBOARD

Athlete Spotlight: True character is often revealed in seasons that test resolve rather than celebrate success. **Candace Parker** encountered moments that could have reshaped her identity. Injuries interrupted momentum, criticism followed her leadership, and the responsibility of carrying a franchise unfolded alongside motherhood. Still, her legacy was not defined by obstacles, but by how she responded to them.

What distinguished Candace was not a chase for recognition, but a commitment to growth. She approached rehabilitation with patience and invested time in developing younger teammates.

Inside locker rooms and team huddles, Candace set a clear standard. Effort mattered. People mattered. Leadership was demonstrated through action, not volume.

Her career reflects the truth that lasting strength forms beneath the surface. She showed that identity rooted in Christ carries greater weight than applause. Athletes can follow that same path by training diligently, speaking honestly, serving their teams, and guarding the heart. Wins eventually fade, but the character you build remains.

PATHWAY TO GROWTH

Personal Reflection: *Where do I usually draw my confidence from right now: how I look, how I perform, or who I am becoming? In what ways might my focus shift if I measured success by character rather than results?*

Faith in Action: This week, place your attention on who you are cultivating, not what you are producing. Choose one intentional action that reflects integrity, humility, or encouragement. Let your daily choices, not the scoreboard, define what success looks like.

Quiet Prayer: God, thank You for valuing my heart above everything others can see. I am grateful that my worth is not tied to performance or recognition. Shape my character, anchor my confidence in You, and help me live with quiet strength that reflects Your truth. **Amen.**

NOTES

27

STRONG, FIRM, STEADFAST

"And the God of all grace, who called you to his eternal glory in Christ, after you have suffered a little while, will himself restore you and make you strong, firm and steadfast."
1 Peter 5:10

Scripture Insight: In 1 Peter 5:10, God offers reassurance that hardship is never wasted. Seasons of struggle are not meant to weaken you permanently, but to prepare you for restoration, strength, and stability that come from Him alone. For athletes, this truth reframes injuries, limited roles, and discouraging seasons as chapters God is actively using to build endurance, confidence, and lasting faith rather than defeat.

MORE THAN THE SCOREBOARD

Athlete Spotlight: Madison Packer has spent much of her professional hockey career learning how resilience is built over time. From season-ending injuries to the ups and downs of women's pro leagues, she has faced setbacks that could have persuaded her to walk away. Instead, she chose the slower route of recovery, patience, and steady discipline.

Madison has spoken openly about how her faith steadies her during long stretches of rehab and transition. She has relied on prayer,

Scripture, and trusted community when mental health challenges surfaced. Rather than letting frustration define those seasons, she leaned on God's presence to restore strength she could not manufacture on her own.

Her journey reflects the truth of 1 Peter 5:10. Restoration often arrives after suffering, and renewed strength is rarely rushed. Through adversity, God shaped a leader who is firm, stable, and equipped to support others. Strength did not simply return to her body. It settled into her character.

PATHWAY TO GROWTH

Personal Reflection: *Which disappointment from my past still weighs on my heart? How could God be using that season to strengthen me rather than define me?*

Faith in Action: Identify one setback you once viewed as failure. This week, intentionally thank God for the growth it may be producing in you. Then take one forward-moving step, whether renewed focus in training, a moment of prayer, or a disciplined choice, and trust Him to continue the work of restoration and strength.

Quiet Prayer: Dear God, thank You for meeting me in moments when I feel worn down or uncertain. I am grateful that You restore what feels broken and steady what feels shaken. Help me move forward with perseverance, confidence, and faith, trusting You to make me strong and secure through every trial. **Amen.**

NOTES

CHAPTER 8: PATIENCE THAT BUILDS PERSEVERANCE

28

TRIAL TO TRIUMPH

"Blessed is the one who perseveres under trial because, having stood the test, that person will receive the crown of life that the Lord has promised to those who love him."
James 1:12

Scripture Insight: Endurance is not overlooked by God. James 1:12 reminds us that perseverance through hardship carries a promise that reaches beyond temporary success. In the life of an athlete, trials such as injury, limited playing time, or long seasons of struggle are not wasted moments. They become spaces where trust deepens and faith is strengthened, shaping character that lasts far longer than any result.

MORE THAN THE SCOREBOARD

Athlete Spotlight: History remembers **Helen Maroulis** for breaking barriers when she earned Olympic gold in wrestling in 2016. What is less visible is the season that followed, when victory was replaced by repeated concussions, intense anxiety, and deep uncertainty. Doctors urged her to step away from the sport, and the future she once knew suddenly felt fragile.

In that difficult stretch, Helen was forced to confront questions far bigger than competition. She turned toward her faith, choosing prayer and dependence on God when physical strength alone was no longer enough. Rather than defining herself by medals, she anchored her identity in something unshakable.

Over time, healing came slowly.

With patience and perseverance, Helen returned to the mat and continued competing at the highest level. Her comeback revealed that true triumph is not measured only by wins, but by the courage to remain faithful when the journey becomes painful. Trials did not end her calling; they refined it and gave it greater depth.

PATHWAY TO GROWTH

Personal Reflection: *What current challenge is testing my patience or resolve? In what ways might God be using this season to strengthen my faith and character?*

Faith in Action: Choose one ongoing challenge and commit it to God daily this week. Before training or competition, read James 1:12 and ask for endurance rather than escape. Take one intentional step that reflects perseverance, whether it is disciplined preparation, honest rest, or focused prayer.

Quiet Prayer: Lord God, I place my trials in Your hands and trust You to use them for good. Give me steady faith when the path feels uncertain and strength to endure with hope. May my perseverance honor You and shape me into who You are calling me to become. **Amen.**

NOTES

29

FAITH THAT MOVES MOUNTAINS

" Truly I tell you, if you have faith as small as a mustard seed, you can say to this mountain, 'Move from here to there,' and it will move. Nothing will be impossible for you."
Matthew 17:20

Scripture Insight: Mountains often appear when circumstances feel overwhelming and progress seems blocked. Matthew 17:20 teaches that God does not require flawless or fearless faith to act on our behalf. Even a small, sincere trust placed in Him can unlock what appears impossible. When faith moves you to take one step forward, God supplies the power that carries the rest.

MORE THAN THE SCOREBOARD

Athlete Spotlight: Some challenges rise far beyond competition, and **Chaunté Lowe** encountered one that no training plan could anticipate. At the peak of her athletic career and with future Olympic goals in sight, she was diagnosed with breast cancer. Treatment drained her strength and clouded her future, leaving her uncertain whether she would ever compete again.

Rather than surrender to fear, Chaunté anchored herself in faith. She turned consistently to prayer and Scripture, trusting that her purpose was greater than results or rankings. Even during chemotherapy, she continued training when possible, choosing perseverance over despair and belief over doubt.

Her journey became a living example of what it means to trust God when the outcome is unknown. Faith did not remove the struggle, but it carried her through it. Chaunté's story reflects the truth that faith empowers endurance, especially when circumstances argue against hope.

PATHWAY TO GROWTH

Personal Reflection: *Where does uncertainty feel heavy in my life right now? Do I respond to fear by pulling back, or by trusting God with what I cannot control? What area am I being invited to place fully in His hands?*

Faith in Action: Set aside a few minutes each day this week to read Matthew 17:20 slowly. Identify one obstacle that feels overwhelming and speak the verse aloud as a prayer. Take one intentional step that reflects trust, whether that means continuing to show up, releasing control, or choosing courage over hesitation.

Quiet Prayer: Lord Jesus, I come to You with the challenges I cannot overcome on my own. Strengthen my faith when fear feels louder than hope and remind me that nothing is impossible with You. Help me walk forward with trust and perseverance in every season. **Amen.**

NOTES

30

ENDURE FOR THE PROMISE

"You need to persevere so that when you have done the will of God, you will receive what he has promised."
Hebrews 10:36

Scripture Insight: God's promises often unfold through persistence rather than immediacy. Hebrews 10:36 reminds us that obedience and endurance go hand in hand with receiving what God has prepared. In the life of an athlete, perseverance may look like continuing through injury, uncertainty, or seasons when progress feels slow. Trusting God's plan requires staying faithful even when results are not yet visible.

MORE THAN THE SCOREBOARD

Athlete Spotlight: Long before success found her, **Stacy Lewis** faced a challenge that could have ended her athletic dreams before they began. As a young golfer, she was diagnosed with scoliosis, a condition that demanded years of wearing a back brace nearly every hour of the day. While others moved freely, her daily life was shaped by restriction and discomfort, followed later by major back surgery.

Even after recovery, doubts lingered about whether she could compete at an elite level. Still, Stacy chose to continue. Rehabilitation demanded patience, and progress required discipline, but she remained committed to the game she loved and to the belief that her journey was not finished.

That perseverance eventually carried her from collegiate golf to the highest stages of the sport. Rising to become the world's top ranked golfer and a major champion, Stacy has consistently pointed to God's faithfulness as the source of her strength. Her story reflects a truth deeper than achievement. Endurance grounded in faith allows God's promises to unfold in ways that shape both skill and character.

PATHWAY TO GROWTH

Personal Reflection: *What ongoing challenge is asking me to remain patient and steady? Where am I tempted to give up before the promise has time to grow? How can I continue trusting God while I wait?*

Faith in Action: Identify one area where perseverance feels difficult right now. Each day this week, read Hebrews 10:36 and ask God for strength to remain faithful. Choose one small, consistent action that reflects commitment rather than discouragement.

Quiet Prayer: Almighty Father, thank You for knowing how heavy perseverance can feel at times. Give me steady courage when progress is slow and help me trust Your promises even when the outcome is unclear. Shape my faith through endurance and let my journey reflect Your faithfulness. **Amen.**

NOTES

31

YOUR HARVEST WILL COME

Let us not become weary in doing good, for at the proper time we will reap a harvest if we do not give up."
Galatians 6:9

Scripture Insight: Faithfulness is often tested in seasons where progress feels invisible. Galatians 6:9 reassures us that weariness does not cancel God's promise, even when results seem delayed. Growth is taking place beneath the surface, shaped by consistency and trust. The call is not to rush the outcome, but to remain steady while God works in His perfect timing.

MORE THAN THE SCOREBOARD

Athlete Spotlight: Waiting on results is rarely easy, especially after early success. **Carli Lloyd** experienced this tension firsthand. After celebrating Olympic gold in 2008, her career entered a challenging stretch marked by injuries, uneven performances, and growing criticism. The momentum she once knew slowed, and the path forward felt uncertain.

Rather than stepping away, she leaned into discipline and faith. Extra training sessions replaced comfort, and rehabilitation demanded patience. During seasons when recognition faded, she stayed committed, trusting that unseen effort still mattered.

That perseverance bore fruit years later on one of the sport's biggest stages.

In the 2015 Women's World Cup final, Carli delivered a performance for the ages, scoring three goals and earning the Golden Ball. What appeared overnight was the result of long obedience, faithful preparation, and belief that God was still at work. Her journey reflects the truth that harvest follows persistence, even when the wait feels long.

PATHWAY TO GROWTH

Personal Reflection: *Where does effort feel unseen or exhausting right now? What habits or disciplines am I tempted to abandon too soon? Which promises from Scripture remind me to keep going?*

Faith in Action: Choose one area where progress feels slow and write it down. Identify two practical ways to remain faithful this week, such as focused training, intentional prayer, or gratitude for small improvements. Release the outcome to God and commit to showing up consistently.

Quiet Prayer: Lord, You see every seed planted in obedience. Strengthen me when patience wears thin and help me trust Your timing when results are delayed. Keep my heart faithful and my spirit hopeful as I wait for the harvest You have promised. **Amen.**

NOTES

CHAPTER 9: COURAGEOUS & CLEAR-MINDED

32

STEADFAST FOR PERFECT PEACE

"You will keep in perfect peace those whose minds are steadfast, because they trust in you."
Isaiah 26:3

Scripture Insight: Peace does not arrive by chance when pressure rises. Isaiah 26:3 reveals that steadiness flows from a mind anchored in trust, not from circumstances lining up perfectly. For an athlete, this kind of calm is cultivated through intention. Fixing your thoughts on God redirects attention away from anxious outcomes and toward the One who remains constant no matter the result.

MORE THAN THE SCOREBOARD

Athlete Spotlight: High pressure moments have a way of exposing what anchors us. **Sloane Stephens** understands this deeply. After a long season interrupted by a serious foot injury, she returned to the sport's biggest stage and captured the 2017 US Open. Competing under intense scrutiny, she relied on consistency rather than emotion to guide her play.

What stands out in Sloane's approach is her commitment to the present moment. Between points, she slows her breathing, repeats her routine, and refuses to let the scoreboard dictate her mindset. In her own words, faith became essential when she walked through a dark and discouraging season and needed God to carry her forward.

That discipline reflects the heart of Isaiah 26:3. Her composure is not passive. It is trained focus built through trust and repetition. When anxiety surfaces, she narrows her attention to what is in front of her and releases the rest. The same choice is available to you. Pressure may show up, but it does not have to control your thoughts, your body, or your performance.

PATHWAY TO GROWTH

Personal Reflection: *Which moments tend to disrupt my calm the most during competition or training? What simple reset can I return to when tension builds? How can I intentionally shift my focus back to Christ in those moments?*

Faith in Action: Select a short phrase from the Scripture and pair it with a steady breath. Practice this reset before each attempt, rep, or play throughout the week. Let it become your signal to release distraction and reengage with purpose and trust.

Quiet Prayer: Dear God, thank You for giving me the peace You promise when my mind is anchored in You. Help me respond to pressure with trust instead of fear and focus instead of noise. Guard my thoughts, steady my heart, and guide my performance with Your calm presence. **Amen.**

NOTES

33

DELIVERED FROM FEAR

"I sought the Lord, and he answered me; he delivered me from all my fears."

Psalm 34:4

Scripture Insight: Fear loses its grip when it is brought into God's presence. Psalm 34:4 reveals that deliverance begins with seeking the Lord rather than trying to manage anxiety on our own. God does not ignore fear or minimize it. He meets us in it and replaces it with freedom. When trust shifts from performance to His faithfulness, fear no longer gets the final word.

MORE THAN THE SCOREBOARD

Athlete Spotlight: Pressure can quietly redefine how an athlete sees herself. In elite softball, where expectations are relentless, **Ali Aguilar** once allowed fear of failure to shape her confidence. Every error felt personal, and every missed opportunity carried weight far beyond the game. Her sense of worth became tangled with outcomes she could not fully control.

Over time, Ali recognized that this mindset was exhausting and limiting. Instead of letting mistakes replay endlessly in her thoughts, she began bringing them to God. Missteps on the field became moments to practice surrender rather than self-criticism. Faith created space for grace to replace fear.

Seeking the Lord changed how Ali competed. Psalm 34:4 became more than a verse; it became a way of thinking. By releasing fear and trusting God with the results, she stepped into competition with clarity and confidence. Her story shows that freedom grows when identity is anchored in God rather than flawless performance.

PATHWAY TO GROWTH

Personal Reflection: *How do I respond internally after a mistake or missed opportunity? What fear tends to surface most often in my performance? What would it look like to release that fear to God instead of carrying it alone?*

Faith in Action: When you catch yourself replaying an error this week, pause and take a steady breath. Pray Psalm 34:4 and remind yourself that fear does not define you. Choose one action that reflects confidence rather than hesitation, whether it is reengaging fully, encouraging a teammate, or trusting your preparation.

Quiet Prayer: Lord, I bring You the fears that surface when I fall short. Help me release the weight of mistakes and remember that my worth is secure in You. Replace fear with courage and allow me to compete with freedom, confidence, and trust in Your care. **Amen.**

NOTES

34

TRAINED FOR RIGHTEOUSNESS

"*No discipline seems pleasant at the time, but painful. Later on, however, it produces a harvest of righteousness and peace for those who have been trained by it.*"
Hebrews 12:11

Scripture Insight: Discipline rarely feels rewarding in the moment it is practiced. Hebrews 12:11 reminds us that growth is often uncomfortable before it is fruitful. God uses consistent training, restraint, and sacrifice to shape both character and faith. When discipline is embraced with purpose, it produces peace and righteousness that last far beyond temporary results.

MORE THAN THE SCOREBOARD

Athlete Spotlight: Colleen Quigley's success in the steeplechase was not built on natural talent alone, but on the unseen hours of training few ever witnessed. Her event demanded repetition, technique work, and patience through long seasons without immediate payoff. Instead of shortcuts, Colleen committed to steady routines that strengthened both mind and body for the moments that mattered.

Her faith has shaped the way she approaches the grind of her sport. Colleen has spoken about finding identity in Christ rather than in times or rankings, which frees her to train with purpose rather than anxiety. The discipline required for elite distance running became an arena where her trust in God matured, especially during injuries and stretches of slow progress.

Colleen's journey illustrates the truth of Hebrews 12:11. Discipline may feel uncomfortable in the moment, but it produces lasting strength and stability. What begins as daily training becomes character that endures beyond competition.

PATHWAY TO GROWTH

Personal Reflection: *Where am I tempted to avoid discipline because it feels uncomfortable or inconvenient? How might God be using consistency and effort to shape my character and faith right now?*

Faith in Action: Choose one habit that supports both physical and spiritual growth and commit to it daily this week. It might be focused preparation, recovery, or intentional prayer. Treat discipline as training for who you are becoming, not just what you are trying to achieve. ou can commit to daily—extra reps, stretching, or prayer before practice. Stick with it, knowing God uses discipline to strengthen both body and soul.

Quiet Prayer: My Lord, I recognize that discipline is part of Your work in my life. Give me patience when training feels difficult and focus when progress feels slow. Shape my habits, my character, and my faith so that they reflect You in every season. **Amen.**

NOTES

35

POWER, LOVE, STRONG MIND

"For God has not given us a spirit of fear, but of power and of love and of a sound mind."
2 Timothy 1:7

Scripture Insight: Fear may speak loudly, but it is not the voice God gives His people. Second Timothy 1:7 makes it clear that anxiety and intimidation do not come from Him. Instead, God supplies strength, love, and disciplined thinking to guide our responses. When pressure rises, this truth invites us to confront fear with confidence rooted in His Spirit rather than our own control.

MORE THAN THE SCOREBOARD

Athlete Spotlight: Confidence on the outside does not always reflect what is happening internally. **Laurie Hernandez** became known worldwide for her joyful expression and fearless routines, yet even she encountered seasons marked by anxiety and mental barriers. After experiencing Olympic success early in her career, she stepped away to confront challenges that training alone could not solve.

Expectations, perfectionism, and fear began to crowd her thoughts. Routines she once performed with ease suddenly felt heavy. Instead of forcing her way through, Laurie turned her attention inward and upward. She leaned into her faith, choosing to anchor her identity in Christ rather than medals or scores.

That shift changed how she approached both competition and life. By trusting God's Word, she learned to quiet fear and steady her mind.

Her story reflects a deeper victory. Mental strength is not built through pressure alone, but through reliance on the power God provides. Fear may surface, but it does not have authority when faith takes the lead.

PATHWAY TO GROWTH

Personal Reflection: *Where do fear or mental hesitation tend to interrupt my performance? What thoughts need to be replaced with God's truth? How can I invite His peace into moments of pressure?*

Faith In Action: When doubt surfaces this week, pause before reacting. Speak 2 Timothy 1:7 aloud and intentionally replace fearful thoughts with words of strength and clarity. Take the next step with focus, trusting God to guide both your mind and your actions.

Quiet Prayer: Dear Lord, Thank You for giving me strength, love, and clarity of mind. When fear tries to take hold, remind me of Your presence and power within me. Help me move forward with confidence, trusting You to steady my thoughts and guide my performance. **Amen.**

NOTES

SECTION III: IMPACT THROUGH TEAMWORK

(WEEKS 36 - 45)

The teams that leave a lasting mark are shaped by more than individual talent. They are formed through trust, humility, unity, and a shared sense of purpose. This section explores how influence grows when athletes choose collaboration over spotlight and commitment over ego.

These devotions focus on serving others well, leading with character, and valuing collective success above personal recognition. Through lessons centered on sacrifice, selflessness, forgiveness, and encouragement, you will learn how to strengthen team culture and reflect Christ in the way you compete, communicate, and support those around you. The result is impact that reaches beyond the field and endures long after the final whistle.

CHAPTER 10: A LIFE OF SELFLESSNESS

36

NO GREATER LOVE

"Greater love has no one than this: to lay down one's life for one's friends."
John 15:13

Scripture Insight: John 15:13 reveals a picture of love that costs something real. Jesus teaches that the deepest form of love is not rooted in words or emotions but in willing surrender for the sake of others. While laying down one's life is the ultimate example, this verse also speaks to everyday sacrifices that place someone else's well-being ahead of personal comfort or recognition.

MORE THAN THE SCOREBOARD

Athlete Spotlight: Allyson Felix is widely celebrated for her dominance on the track, yet her most powerful victory did not come with a medal. After becoming a mother, she encountered an unsettling reality in professional sports: female athletes were often penalized or dismissed from sponsorships for starting families.

Rather than choosing security, she chose conviction. Allyson publicly challenged Nike's maternity policies, fully aware that speaking out could cost her financial stability and endorsements. Still, she pressed forward, determined to protect the dignity and rights of women in sport.

That sacrifice carried weight. Though she lost major sponsorship income, her advocacy sparked change across the industry and opened doors for countless athletes who came after her. Eventually, she partnered with Athleta and launched her own footwear line, a reminder that surrendering something for the right reason can lead to impact far greater than personal gain.

Allyson's journey reveals that being a champion is not defined only by success on the field, but by the choices made when standing up for others costs something personal. Influence matters most when it is used in service, not self-protection.

PATHWAY TO GROWTH

Personal Reflection: *What am I holding tightly that God may be asking me to release? Where can I choose selflessness instead of comfort? Do my actions reflect love for others or a desire for recognition?*

Faith in Action: Identify one opportunity this week to put someone else first. That may mean adjusting your schedule to support a teammate, offering encouragement without expecting anything in return, or stepping aside so another person can grow. Choose a response that reflects love through action, not convenience.

Quiet Prayer: Heavenly Father, thank You for the example of sacrificial love shown through Jesus. I am grateful for the ways You invite me to love beyond myself. Help me recognize moments where I can serve with humility and courage. Shape my heart to reflect Your love in both small choices and bold decisions. **Amen.**

NOTES

37

WE OVER ME, ALWAYS

"Do nothing out of selfish ambition or vain conceit. Rather, in humility value others above yourselves."
Philippians 2:3

Scripture Insight: Philippians 2:3 speaks directly to the tension between pride and humility. This verse invites us to examine our motives and shift our focus away from self-promotion toward honoring others. God's call is clear: true strength is revealed when ambition takes a back seat to service and humility shapes the way we compete and lead.

MORE THAN THE SCOREBOARD

Athlete Spotlight: In elite-level volleyball, where recognition often follows the final point, **Courtney Thompson** built her reputation in a very different way. As a two-time Olympian with Team USA, she was rarely chasing attention. Instead, she devoted herself to a role that required vision, trust, and sacrifice. As a setter, her success depended on helping others perform at their best.

Each match became an exercise in humility. Courtney measured achievement not by personal statistics but by the confidence and rhythm of her teammates. Her precise sets, calm presence, and consistent encouragement turned the spotlight outward, allowing others to thrive in key moments.

That mindset carried beyond the court. In conversations and interviews, Courtney routinely highlighted her teammates' contributions and spoke openly about the importance of unity. She understood that volleyball is built on connection, and her responsibility was to strengthen the whole team, not elevate herself.

Her example shows that choosing others does not mean diminishing your value. It means embracing your role fully and serving with purpose. Influence grows when ego fades, and leadership becomes most powerful when it is rooted in humility.

PATHWAY TO GROWTH

Personal Reflection: *Where do I feel tempted to seek recognition instead of collaboration? How can I support others more intentionally in my current role? do I honor my contribution even when it goes unnoticed?*

Faith in Action: This week, look for intentional ways to elevate someone else. That might involve offering encouragement during a tough moment, recognizing a teammate's effort publicly, or quietly supporting their growth without expecting credit. Practice leadership that strengthens the group, not just the individual.

Quiet Prayer: God, thank You for reminding me that humility reflects Your heart. I am grateful for the teammates and opportunities You place in my life. Teach me to serve with joy, release the need for recognition, and value others with sincerity. May my actions point beyond myself and honor You. **Amen.**

NOTES

38

MORE THAN THE GAME

"For to me, to live is Christ and to die is gain."
Philippians 1:21

Scripture Insight: Philippians 1:21 draws a clear line between what drives our lives and what simply fills our time. Paul's words remind us that real life is found when Christ becomes the center of everything we pursue, including competition and ambition. When faith shapes purpose, success is no longer measured by outcomes alone but by obedience and devotion.

MORE THAN THE SCOREBOARD

Athlete Spotlight: While many athletes focus on recognition and records, **Kenzie Koerber** chose a different definition of success. She had already built an impressive volleyball résumé during her college career, earning national accolades and attention, yet her most meaningful decision had nothing to do with awards.

After thriving at the University of Utah, Kenzie made a choice that surprised many. She transferred to BYU not to elevate her profile, but to strengthen her walk with God and compete alongside teammates who shared her faith-centered purpose. Stepping into unfamiliar territory required courage, yet she understood that following Christ often involves leaving comfort behind.

That commitment shaped how she led. Kenzie became known for encouragement, mentorship, and steady faith in both victory and disappointment. Her confidence did not come from statistics or applause but from her identity in Christ.

Her story illustrates what it means to live beyond personal gain. When God's calling becomes the priority, ambition is not eliminated, it is refined. Influence then extends far beyond the court, and purpose remains steady regardless of results.

PATHWAY TO GROWTH

Personal Reflection: *Where has my focus shifted toward personal recognition instead of God's purpose? How can my role create space for faith to lead? What would it look like to fully dedicate this season to something greater than myself?*

Faith in Action: Choose one intentional act this week that reflects a Christ-centered mindset. Offer guidance to a teammate, speak encouragement during a challenging moment, or step back so someone else can grow. Let your decisions show that your purpose reaches beyond performance.

Quiet Prayer: My Lord, thank You for inviting me into a life that goes beyond wins and losses. I am grateful for the opportunity to use my sport as a place of worship and service. Help me keep You at the center, love my teammates well, and honor You in every moment. **Amen.**

NOTES

CHAPTER 11: LEAD WITH IMPACT

39

SILENCE THE NOISE

"If it is possible, as far as it depends on you, live at peace with everyone."
Romans 12:18

Scripture Insight: Romans 12:18 calls believers to actively pursue peace in their relationships. This instruction recognizes that conflict will arise, yet it places responsibility on our responses rather than others' behavior. For athletes, this verse challenges us to reject division, comparison, and unnecessary tension, choosing instead actions and words that reflect God's calming presence.

MORE THAN THE SCOREBOARD

Athlete Spotlight: In the intense environment of international soccer, where pressure and personalities often collide, **Tobin Heath** became known for more than technical brilliance. Her creativity on the field was matched by a grounded, steady demeanor off it. While others were drawn into comparison or locker room tension, Tobin consistently remained focused on purpose and unity.

That posture did not happen by accident. Tobin has spoken openly about rooting her identity in Christ, a foundation that allowed her to rise above distractions and emotional noise. Instead of feeding gossip or rivalry, she invested in authentic relationships and maintained a team-first mindset.

When challenges surfaced, she chose restraint over reaction. Conversations were redirected, encouragement was offered freely, and her actions reflected humility rather than ego. In moments when drama could have gained momentum, her calm leadership protected trust and cohesion.

Her example demonstrates that strength does not require dominance. Peace-building is a form of leadership, and quiet consistency often speaks louder than confrontation. Competitive drive and Christlike character can coexist when unity becomes the priority.

PATHWAY TO GROWTH

Personal Reflection: *How do my words and reactions influence the atmosphere around me? Where might God be inviting me to respond with peace instead of emotion? Who could benefit from my encouragement or steady presence right now?*

Faith in Action: Make a conscious effort this week to reduce noise rather than add to it. Speak life during tense moments, step away from negative conversations, and support someone quietly without drawing attention. Let your leadership be felt through consistency and calm.

Quiet Prayer: Dear God, thank You for placing me in environments where I can grow in both character and faith. I am grateful for the opportunity to represent You through my actions. Help me choose peace, guard my words, and reflect Your love in every interaction. **Amen.**

NOTES

40

SHEPHERD YOUR TEAM

"Be shepherds of God's flock that is under your care, watching over them—not because you must, but because you are willing... not lording it over those entrusted to you, but being examples to the flock."
1 Peter 5:2–3

Scripture Insight: In this verse, leadership is reframed as responsibility rather than authority. This passage emphasizes care, willingness, and example over control or status. God's design for leadership centers on influence shaped by humility, where actions speak louder than titles.

MORE THAN THE SCOREBOARD

Athlete Spotlight: Strong leadership is not measured only by visibility but by consistency and character. **Elana Meyers Taylor** has demonstrated this truth throughout her career. As one of the most accomplished women in bobsledding, she earned five Olympic medals, yet her impact extended far beyond competition results.

As captain of Team USA, Elana embraced leadership through service. She trained relentlessly, held herself to high standards, and supported newer teammates as they found their footing. Her presence set the tone not through command, but through commitment.

Off the track, Elana used her voice to advocate for fairness, inclusion, and respect within athletics. Open about her faith, she shared her desire to honor God in every area of life, a principle that shaped both her influence and decisions. Her leadership mirrored the heart of 1 Peter 5:2–3. She led because she cared deeply, not because of obligation or position. Influence flowed from example rather than authority.

Elana's story reminds athletes that anchoring a team means stepping forward during difficult moments, modeling humility, and creating an environment where others feel supported. True leadership leaves a lasting imprint not through recognition, but through service and faithfulness.

PATHWAY TO GROWTH

Personal Reflection: *What kind of example do my daily actions set? Do I lead with patience and care, or wait for acknowledgment? Where can I choose service over comfort this week?*

Faith in Action: Practice leadership through simple, intentional acts. Offer encouragement to someone who feels overlooked, take initiative in supporting team needs, or quietly pray for a teammate facing pressure. Help a struggling teammate or pray for someone on your team. Let your actions speak louder than words.

Quiet Prayer: Lord, thank You for entrusting me with opportunities to lead and serve. I am grateful for the people You place in my care. Shape my heart to reflect humility, courage, and faithfulness so my example points others toward You. **Amen.**

NOTES

41

SHINE TO LEAD

"Let your light shine before others, that they may see your good deeds and glorify your Father in heaven."
Matthew 5:16

Scripture Insight: Matthew 5:16 shifts the purpose of influence away from self-promotion and toward God's glory. Jesus teaches that the light within us is meant to illuminate His goodness, not draw attention to ourselves. When faith shapes our actions, leadership becomes a reflection of God's character rather than a pursuit of recognition.

MORE THAN THE SCOREBOARD

Athlete Spotlight: True leadership often appears quieter than the world expects. **Kelly Clark** demonstrated this throughout her historic snowboarding career. A five-time Olympian and gold medalist, she reached heights few athletes ever experience, yet her influence extended well beyond podium finishes.

Early in her career, Kelly overheard a comment from a peer that reshaped her perspective: God's love was not dependent on winning. That moment marked the beginning of a deeper faith that transformed how she competed, related to others, and viewed success.

Kelly has become known for encouragement and humility. She invested in those around her, celebrated others' achievements, and carried a calm confidence rooted in Christ rather than comparison. Her leadership showed up through consistency, kindness, and how she treated people under pressure.

She lived out Matthew 5:16 not by drawing attention to herself, but by allowing her faith to quietly influence her choices. Her example reminds us that character leaves a longer legacy than medals ever could. For female athletes seeking to lead well, Kelly's story offers clarity. Light shines brightest through humility, service, and integrity. Influence grows when actions point upward instead of inward.

PATHWAY TO GROWTH

Personal Reflection: *What does my leadership reveal about where my confidence comes from? How do my responses under pressure reflect my faith? Where can I intentionally allow God's light to shape my influence?*

Faith in Action: Choose one way to lead through example this week. Offer sincere encouragement, support someone who feels overlooked, or serve without expecting acknowledgment.

Quiet Prayer: Lord, thank You for placing Your light within me. I'm grateful for the opportunity to influence others through my actions. Help me lead with humility, serve with sincerity, and reflect Your goodness so that everything I do brings You honor. **Amen.**

NOTES

42

MIRROR HIS WAYS

"Follow my example, as I follow the example of Christ."
1 Corinthians 11:1

Scripture Insight: In 1 Corinthians 11:1, Paul reminds Christians that influence begins with imitation. Leadership is not about directing attention to yourself but about modeling a life shaped by Christ. When actions reflect His character, others are naturally guided toward Him through example rather than instruction.

MORE THAN THE SCOREBOARD

Athlete Spotlight: Impactful leadership often extends far beyond competition. **Natasha Watley** has lived this truth throughout and beyond her playing career. As one of the most accomplished softball athletes in the United States, she earned Olympic gold and silver medals and helped elevate the visibility of women in the sport. Still, her legacy reaches further than athletic achievement.

After stepping away from elite competition, Natasha chose to invest intentionally in others. Through the Natasha Watley Foundation, she began mentoring female athletes by combining skill development with confidence-building and faith-centered values. Her approach to leadership was never about authority or status, but about connection and service.

Rather than separating herself from those she mentors, Natasha walks alongside them. She teaches by example, demonstrating what it looks like to lead with humility, purpose, and compassion. Her influence reflects the heart of 1 Corinthians 11:1 by pointing people toward Christ through daily actions.

Her journey illustrates that leadership is not defined by titles or accomplishments. It is shaped by a willingness to serve, encourage, and guide others with sincerity. When success is shared instead of guarded, it becomes a tool for lasting impact.

PATHWAY TO GROWTH

Personal Reflection: *How does my behavior reflect Christ in everyday situations? Where can I choose service over recognition? Who might God be inviting me to encourage or support right now?*

Faith in Action: Look for a practical way to lead through service this week. Offer help without being asked, encourage someone who may feel overlooked, or give your time to support a teammate's growth. Let your example speak louder than your words.

Quiet Prayer: Lord, thank You for the leaders who have shown me what it looks like to follow You. I am grateful for the opportunity to influence others through my actions. Teach me to lead with humility, serve with joy, and reflect Christ in everything I do. **Amen.**

NOTES

CHAPTER 12: ONE TEAM, ONE PURPOSE

43

UNITED IN CHRIST

"For where two or three gather in my name, there am I with them."

Matthew 18:20

Scripture Insight: Matthew 18:20 offers reassurance that God's presence is not dependent on numbers or settings. Jesus makes it clear that when believers come together with hearts focused on Him, He is already there. Unity rooted in faith invites strength and purpose into the simplest moments.

MORE THAN THE SCOREBOARD

Athlete Spotlight: Sustained excellence is rarely built on talent alone. The **University of Oklahoma Sooners softball** have established themselves as one of the most dominant programs in collegiate athletics, yet their foundation runs deeper than performance. Central to their culture is a shared commitment to faith and togetherness.

Before and after competition, teammates often gather in prayer, not to demand outcomes, but to acknowledge God's presence and express gratitude for the opportunity to compete. These moments reflect a mindset that values purpose over pressure and connection over comparison.

Players such as Jocelyn Alo and Grace Lyons have spoken openly about how faith shapes the team's identity. They consistently point to a collective mission that extends beyond championships. Glorifying God, supporting one another, and maintaining perspective during high-stakes moments remain central priorities.

Leadership within the program reinforces this approach by emphasizing family, trust, and accountability. Success is celebrated, but unity is protected through both victories and challenges. Their shared faith has become a stabilizing force that keeps the team grounded regardless of the scoreboard. For Oklahoma softball, gathering in prayer is more than habit. It is a declaration that Christ is at the center of everything they pursue. Their example reminds athletes that inviting God into team spaces does not require elaborate words. Presence, intention, and unity are enough.

PATHWAY TO GROWTH

Personal Reflection: *How do I invite God into my team environment? Where can I take initiative to encourage unity right now?*

Faith in Action: Look for an opportunity to foster spiritual unity. Invite teammates to pray briefly before or after practice, or pause to thank God together following competition. Even small moments of shared faith can strengthen trust and alignment.

Quiet Prayer: God, thank You for the teammates You place in my life and the opportunity to walk in faith together. I am grateful for Your presence when we gather in Your name. Draw our hearts closer to You and to one another in all we do. **Amen.**

NOTES

44

ONE SPIRIT, ONE FIGHT

"Whatever happens, conduct yourselves in a manner worthy of the gospel of Christ. Then, whether I come and see you or only hear about you in my absence, I will know that you stand firm in the one Spirit, striving together as one for the faith of the gospel."

Philippians 1:27

Scripture Insight: Philippians 1:27 calls believers to live in a way that reflects the gospel through unity and purpose. Paul emphasizes standing firm together, not allowing pride or personal ambition to fracture the group. A life worthy of Christ is marked by shared commitment where faith shapes how people work, compete, and support one another.

MORE THAN THE SCOREBOARD

Athlete Spotlight: Championship programs are built on more than talent. **Nebraska Cornhuskers volleyball** has long been rooted in togetherness, discipline, and shared values. While their success is visible in titles and banners, the foundation of their excellence is found in how they operate as one unit.

Within the program, individual recognition is secondary to collective responsibility. Athletes are encouraged to celebrate each other's success, push one another toward growth, and show up fully for the team every day.

That unity extends beyond competition. Prayer and reflection are woven into the rhythm of the team, reinforcing that their purpose goes beyond winning matches. Faith helps anchor their identity, reminding them that how they compete matters as much as the outcome.

Nebraska volleyball demonstrates what can happen when athletes share one mission. Trust deepens, confidence grows, and the impact reaches further than the scoreboard.

PATHWAY TO GROWTH

Personal Reflection: *Where do I prioritize my own goals over the good of the team? How can I strengthen unity through my attitude and actions? What would it look like to fully commit to a shared mission right now?*

Faith in Action: This week reinforce team unity. Offer encouragement during a difficult moment, pray for a teammate facing pressure, or choose to support the group even when personal recognition is absent. Let your actions reflect a commitment to something bigger than yourself.

Quiet Prayer: Father, thank You for my teammates. I am grateful for the strength that comes from unity. Teach me to put the mission You've given us above personal ambition and to compete with a spirit that honors You in every moment. **Amen.**

NOTES

45

HONOR YOUR SISTERS

"Be devoted to one another in love. Honor one another above yourselves."
Romans 12:10

Scripture Insight: Romans 12:10 reframes competition through the lens of love and devotion. This verse challenges believers to place the needs, growth, and dignity of others ahead of personal recognition. When honor replaces ego, teamwork becomes an expression of faith rather than a pursuit of individual success.

MORE THAN THE SCOREBOARD

Athlete Spotlight: Championship teams are often defined by talent, but lasting legacies are built through unity. **The Baylor Bears women's basketball team** exemplified this truth during their national championship run, fueled not only by execution and defense, but by a deep commitment to serving one another with humility and shared purpose.

That culture became especially visible through the leadership of players such as Chloe Jackson and Kalani Brown. When the team needed stability at point guard, Chloe stepped into the role despite joining the program for just one season, embracing responsibility without seeking attention.

Her willingness to adapt became a turning point. Chloe's selfless mindset helped anchor the group, and her game-winning shot in the national championship symbolized the power of playing for something greater than self.

Baylor's emphasis on prayer, humility, and servant leadership shaped more than their season. Their example shows that honoring teammates builds trust that carries through pressure-filled moments and creates impact that reaches beyond the final score.

PATHWAY TO GROWTH

Personal Reflection: *Where can I choose service instead of recognition? How do my actions show honor toward those I compete alongside? What would it look like to place team unity above personal goals this week?*

Faith in Action: Take an intentional step to honor a teammate. Send a message of encouragement, offer support during a challenging moment, or pray specifically for someone else's strength and confidence. Let your actions reflect devotion and Christ-centered love. send a prayer to one teammate. Whether she's struggling or shining, show her what it looks like to love with Christ-like humility and put others first.

Quiet Prayer: Jesus, thank You for surrounding me with teammates who walk this journey alongside me. I am grateful for the opportunity to grow through community. Teach me to love selflessly, serve with humility, and honor others above myself in every setting. **Amen.**

NOTES

SECTION IV: CHRIST-LIKE CHARACTER

(WEEKS 46 - 52)

A lasting legacy in your sport is shaped by far more than numbers on a stat sheet or scoreboard. It is revealed through the way Christ is reflected in daily choices, quiet moments, and unseen decisions. This section encourages female athletes to live with conviction, extend forgiveness freely, and lead with humility, even when recognition is absent.

Through examples rooted in grace, sacrifice, perseverance, and unwavering faith, these devotions encourage you to become a steady light for Christ within your sport. As character deepens, influence expands. By aligning words, actions, and attitude with Christ's example, you learn how to compete with integrity and carry your witness well beyond the field, court, or arena.

CHAPTER 13: GRACE THAT FORGIVES

46

PLAY WITH A FORGIVING HEART

"Bear with each other and forgive one another if any of you has a grievance against someone. Forgive as the Lord forgave you."
Colossians 3:13

Scripture Insight: Colossians 3:13 places forgiveness at the center of a Christ-centered life. This verse reminds us that grace is not reserved for easy moments, but for situations that test patience and humility. Forgiving as Christ forgave means choosing mercy even when emotions push us toward resentment.

MORE THAN THE SCOREBOARD

Athlete Spotlight: Few athletes have entered professional competition under a brighter spotlight than **Caitlin Clark**. Her rookie season brought constant attention, sold-out arenas, and defenders determined to challenge her at every turn. With that visibility came intense physical play, sharp criticism, and moments that demanded emotional restraint.

Rather than reacting out of frustration, Caitlin chose composure, staying focused on growth and letting her performance speak for itself. That decision required discipline when contact felt excessive or reactions seemed unfair.

By refusing retaliation, she demonstrated strength guided by self-control and refused to let anger dictate her actions or derail her purpose. Caitlin's approach shows that forgiveness often happens in real time, especially when emotions run high and pressure is relentless.

Choosing forgiveness does not diminish competitiveness. It elevates it, sharpening focus and replacing distraction with peace. That posture reveals Christ's work in the heart far more clearly than any reaction ever could.

PATHWAY TO GROWTH

Personal Reflection: *How do I respond when I feel disrespected or treated unfairly? What would forgiveness look like in the moment rather than later?*
Is there a situation where I need to release frustration right now?

Faith in Action: The next time tension rises, pause before responding. Take a breath, recall Colossians 3:13, and choose a calm, measured reaction. Let grace guide your response so your actions reflect Christ rather than emotion.

Quiet Prayer: Jesus, thank You for the forgiveness You have shown me so freely. I am grateful for the grace You extend even when I fall short. Teach me to forgive with courage and humility so my responses reflect Your love in every situation. **Amen.**

NOTES

47

RISE AFTER THE FALL

"For though the righteous fall seven times, they rise again."
Proverbs 24:16

Scripture Insight: Proverbs 24:16 speaks less about perfection and more about perseverance. God does not promise a path without missteps, but He does promise strength to rise again. This verse reminds us that resilience rooted in faith allows setbacks to become moments of growth rather than endpoints.

MORE THAN THE SCOREBOARD

Athlete Spotlight: Few moments test an athlete's resolve like failure on a public stage. **Erin Jackson** encountered that reality during the 2022 U.S. Olympic trials. A stumble during her race cost her a qualifying spot, and in an instant, years of preparation appeared to slip away. What followed was unexpected. In an extraordinary act of selflessness, her teammate Brittany Bowe chose to give up her own Olympic place so Erin could compete. That moment shifted the story from disappointment to opportunity.

Erin refused to let one mistake define her journey. She regrouped, stayed focused, and stepped onto the Olympic stage with renewed determination. Weeks later, she made history by becoming the first Black woman to win an Olympic gold medal in speedskating.

Her story reflects the truth of Proverbs 24:16. Falling did not disqualify her. Rising with faith, humility, and resolve revealed her strength. What looked like an ending became the beginning of something greater.

For athletes navigating pressure and expectation, Erin's experience offers perspective. Missed opportunities, losses, and errors are part of the journey. They do not determine identity or future. The response matters more than the stumble itself.

PATHWAY TO GROWTH

Personal Reflection: *How do I usually respond when I fall short of expectations? What helps me refocus after a mistake? Where do I need to trust God to help me rise again this week?*

Faith in Action: When a setback occurs, pause and acknowledge it without judgment. Reflect on Proverbs 24:16, then identify one constructive step you can take forward. Growth often begins with a single intentional response.

Quiet Prayer: Dear God, thank You for the strength You provide when I fall. I am grateful that You do not define me by my mistakes. Help me rise with confidence, learn from setbacks, and trust You to guide every step forward. **Amen.**

NOTES

48

ALL THINGS THROUGH CHRIST

"I can do all this through him who gives me strength."
Philippians 4:13

Scripture Insight: Philippians 4:13 speaks to a deeper kind of strength than outward success. This verse reminds us that God's power sustains us not only in moments of victory, but also when expectations collapse or results disappoint. Living this truth means depending on Christ for steadiness, humility, and endurance regardless of outcome.

MORE THAN THE SCOREBOARD

Athlete Spotlight: Madison Keys has been open about how her Christian faith steadies her through the highs and lows of professional tennis. Major finals, heartbreaking losses, injuries, and rankings swings have all tested her resolve. Instead of finding strength in results, Madison has repeatedly drawn attention to her faith as the anchor that keeps her grounded.

One defining moment came after her defeat in the 2017 US Open final, a match filled with expectation and pressure. Though falling short of the title, she embraced her opponent, Sloane Stephens, congratulated her publicly, and later spoke about choosing gratitude over frustration. Her response reflected the humility and perspective of someone who sees strength as something received, not manufactured.

Throughout her career, Madison has credited God for the abilities she has been given and has spoken about the importance of competing with joy rather than fear. Her example aligns with Philippians 4:13.

Strength through Christ becomes visible not only in victories, but in how one carries disappointment with grace, confidence, and peace that does not depend on the scoreboard.

PATHWAY TO GROWTH

Personal Reflection: *How do I usually respond when results fall short of expectations? What would it look like to rely on God's strength in disappointment? Where can I practice grace instead of frustration this week?*

Faith in Action: After a setback or mistake, choose a response that reflects Christ. Offer encouragement to someone else, thank a coach or official, or pause to pray before reacting. Let your composure speak louder than the outcome.

Quiet Prayer: Father, thank You for being my strength in every season. I am grateful that You walk with me through both success and disappointment. Teach me to respond with humility, patience, and trust so my life reflects Your presence no matter the result. **Amen.**

NOTES

CHAPTER 14: WITNESS THROUGH ACTION

49

NEVER ASHAMED

"For I am not ashamed of the gospel, because it is the power of God that brings salvation to everyone who believes."
Romans 1:16

Scripture Insight: Romans 1:16 is a bold declaration of confidence in the gospel's power. Paul reminds believers that faith is not something to downplay or keep hidden, even when it draws attention or criticism. Living unashamed means allowing God's truth to shape both conviction and conduct, regardless of the setting.

MORE THAN THE SCOREBOARD

Athlete Spotlight: Olympic competition brings global scrutiny, and hurdler and bobsledder **Lolo Jones** has navigated that stage with transparency about her faith in Christ. While her accomplishments spanned multiple Olympic cycles and two sports, her boldness about what grounded her made her stand out even more.

Throughout her career, Lolo spoke openly about prayer, Scripture, and her dependence on God in both victory and disappointment. She consistently reminded audiences that her identity was not defined by medals or headlines, but by her relationship with Christ. That conviction guided how she processed injury, pressure, and high expectations.

Her openness sometimes drew criticism and misinterpretation, yet she chose not to retreat or soften her beliefs for public approval. Instead, she lived out her faith with clarity and gratitude, allowing others to see Christ through her responses on and off the track.

Lolo's story reflects the heart of Romans 1:16. Being unashamed of the gospel is not about perfection or spotlight moments—it is about confidence in Christ that remains steady under pressure. Influence grows when faith is lived publicly, humbly, and without apology.

PATHWAY TO GROWTH

Personal Reflection: *Where do I feel pressure to stay silent about my faith? What would it look like to live more openly for Christ in my environment? How can I give God recognition through my actions this week?*

Faith in Action: Choose one intentional moment to reflect your faith openly. That may be offering a prayer before competition, expressing gratitude to God after a result, or sharing encouragement rooted in Scripture. Let your actions point clearly to the source of your strength.

Quiet Prayer: God, thank You for the courage You give to stand firm in truth. I am grateful for examples of faith lived boldly. Help me walk with confidence, remain rooted in You, and reflect Your light without fear in every place I compete and live. **Amen.**

NOTES

50

COUNTER THE CULTURE

"Do not conform to the pattern of this world, but be transformed by the renewing of your mind."
Romans 12:2

Scripture Insight: Romans 12:2 challenges believers to resist cultural pressure and allow Christ to reshape the way they think and live. Transformation begins in the mind and becomes visible through choices that reflect God's truth rather than popular opinion.

MORE THAN THE SCOREBOARD

Athlete Spotlight: Standing apart is rarely easy, especially in competitive environments that reward image, popularity, and recognition. **Jennie Finch** chose a different path throughout her career. As an Olympic gold medalist and one of the most recognizable names in softball, she carried immense influence, yet she consistently used that platform to reflect her faith rather than chase approval.

Jennie was open about her commitment to Christ in interviews, personal interactions, and mentorship. She incorporated Scripture into autograph signings and conversations, reminding others that her identity was rooted in faith, not performance.

That mindset shaped how she competed and led. Jennie showed that excellence and conviction are not opposing forces. By choosing values over validation, she demonstrated that success does not require conforming to every trend or expectation.

Her influence continued long after her playing days. Through speaking, coaching, and encouraging athletes to ground their worth in Christ rather than comparison, Jennie challenges the next generation to live with intention. Her life reflects the heart of Romans 12:2, proving that lasting impact comes from transformation rather than imitation.

PATHWAY TO GROWTH

Personal Reflection: *Where do I feel pressure to compromise my values? How might renewing my mind reshape my daily choices? What opportunity do I have to reflect Christ more clearly right now?*

Faith in Action: Choose one intentional way to live differently this week. Speak with kindness when negativity is expected, encourage someone who feels overlooked, or begin a practice or competition with prayer. Let your actions show that transformation is already at work within you.

Quiet Prayer: Heavenly Father, thank You for renewing my mind and shaping my heart. I am grateful that You call me to a life guided by truth rather than trends. Help me resist pressure to conform and live with courage, humility, and purpose so my life points others to You. **Amen.**

NOTES

51

HUMBLE & EXALTED

"Humble yourselves before the Lord, and he will lift you up."
James 4:10

Scripture Insight: James 4:10 turns the world's definition of success upside down. Instead of chasing elevation through recognition or achievement, this verse invites us to lower ourselves before God in trust and surrender. When humility leads the way, God becomes the One who defines timing, promotion, and purpose.

MORE THAN THE SCOREBOARD

Athlete Spotlight: Dominance in sport often brings attention, praise, and pressure to self-promote. **Katie Ledecky** has experienced all of it. With multiple Olympic gold medals and world records to her name, she stands among the most accomplished athletes in swimming history. Yet what consistently sets her apart is not only how she wins, but how she carries success.

After races, Katie's focus rarely turns inward. Gratitude comes first. She openly thanks God, acknowledges her coaches, and recognizes the teammates who helped shape her journey. Even when the spotlight is firmly on her, she redirects it with intention and grace.

That posture reflects a deeper conviction. Katie has shared that she does her best and entrusts the outcome to God, anchoring her identity in faith rather than medals. Her confidence is steady, not loud. Her victories are powerful, yet marked by composure and humility.

Her example shows that excellence and humility are not in conflict. They strengthen one another. By refusing to cling to recognition, she demonstrates that success is safest when held loosely and credited rightly. Katie's legacy reaches beyond record books. It lives in the way she honors God through discipline, gratitude, and restraint. True greatness does not demand attention. It reflects character shaped by faith.

PATHWAY TO GROWTH

Personal Reflection: *How do I respond internally when I experience success? Where might God be inviting me to practice humility right now? What does giving God the credit look like in my daily routine?*

Faith in Action: The next time something goes well, pause before celebrating yourself. Express gratitude out loud. Thank God, recognize someone who supported you, or quietly acknowledge the source of the opportunity. Let humility guide your response.

Quiet Prayer: Lord, thank You for the gifts and opportunities You place in my life. I am grateful for every chance to grow and succeed. Teach me to remain humble, give You the glory, and reflect Christlike character in every victory. **Amen.**

NOTES

52

YOUR GAME, HIS WITNESS

"But you will receive power when the Holy Spirit comes on you; and you will be my witnesses in Jerusalem, and in all Judea and Samaria, and to the ends of the earth."
Acts 1:8

Scripture Insight: Acts 1:8 makes it clear that being a witness is not limited to certain places or platforms. Jesus promises power through the Holy Spirit so believers can represent Him wherever they are sent, including competitive environments and moments under pressure where faith is revealed through conduct and response.

MORE THAN THE SCOREBOARD

Athlete Spotlight: Christen Press became known for her composure and creativity as a forward on the U.S. Women's National Team. Competing on the world's biggest stages placed her under intense pressure, yet her steadiness reflected a confidence rooted in Christ rather than circumstances.

For Christen, witness began with identity. She has spoken openly about finding worth in Jesus instead of in goals, roster spots, or public opinion. That perspective shaped how she competed, allowing her to play with freedom and treat others with kindness and respect.

Faith also guided how she used her platform off the field. She served teammates, supported younger athletes, and used her influence for causes centered on hope and empowerment.

Her example shows that witness does not always sound like a speech. Sometimes it looks like humility after a win, gratitude after a loss, and strength guided by faith. Through her sport, Christen demonstrated that faith can be lived publicly and consistently, allowing Christ to be seen through both character and conduct.

PATHWAY TO GROWTH

Personal Reflection: *How do my actions during competition reflect what I believe? Where can I be more intentional about representing Christ through my attitude? What does a faithful witness look like in my current season?*

Faith in Action: Be intentional this week about reflecting Christ through behavior rather than words. Encourage someone who is discouraged, respond calmly after a mistake, or openly express gratitude to God after competition.

Quiet Prayer: Gracious Lord, thank You for placing me exactly where I am. I am grateful for the opportunity to represent You through my sport. Help me compete with humility, courage, and faith so that others see Your character reflected in my life. **Amen.**

NOTES

WHERE YOUR LEGACY BEGINS

As this devotional comes to a close, your calling as an athlete continues. This faith-fueled path was never about achievements, recognition, or reaching a finish line. It was about becoming someone whose faith is visible through competition, character, and everyday choices.

True greatness is not defined by wins or statistics. It is revealed in how you lead under pressure, encourage others, serve selflessly, forgive freely, persevere through adversity, and honor God through your sport.

Across these pages, you encountered women who faced pressure, setbacks, self-doubt, and criticism, yet chose to trust God in both victory and defeat. Whether the spotlight was bright or completely absent, they remained anchored in Him.

As one season ends and another begins, remember that your faith remains your greatest advantage. Open your Bible before you train. Pray before you compete. Encourage the teammate who needs support. Compete with integrity, even when no one is watching.

Let this devotional be the beginning of a life shaped by faith, purpose, and Christlike character, reaching far beyond the field and into every area of your life. May God continue to guide your every step. God Bless.

SCRIPTURE SOURCES

Throughout this devotional, Scripture passages are presented from a variety of Bible translations to enhance understanding and strengthen each message. The translations included are the New International Version (NIV), English Standard Version (ESV), and New Living Translation (NLT). These verses were thoughtfully selected to clearly convey biblical truth in a way that connects with female athletes today.

Biblica, Inc. (2011). *The Holy Bible: New International Version*. (Original work published 1973). Biblica, Inc.

Crossway. (2001). *The Holy Bible: English Standard Version*. Crossway Bibles.

Tyndale House Foundation. (2015). *The Holy Bible: New Living Translation*. (Original work published 1996). Tyndale House Publishers, Inc.

www.ingramcontent.com/pod-product-compliance
Lightning Source LLC
LaVergne TN
LVHW010108170826
845678LV00012B/2301
9781968213107